AI
Driverless Cars
Potentiality

Practical Advances in
Artificial Intelligence and Machine Learning

Dr. Lance B. Eliot, MBA, PhD

DEDICATION

To my incredible daughter, Lauren, and my incredible son, Michael.
Forest fortuna adiuvat (from the Latin; good fortune favors the brave).

CONTENTS

Acknowledgments iii

Introduction 1

Chapters

1 Eliot Framework for AI Self-Driving Cars 15

2 Russian Values and AI Self-Driving Cars 29

3 Friendships Uplift and AI Self-Driving Cars 43

4 Dogs Driving and AI Self-Driving Cars 57

5 Hypodermic Needles and AI Self-Driving Cars 73

6 Sharing Self-Driving Tech Is Not Likely 87

7 Uber Driver "Kidnapper" Is Self-Driving Car Lesson 101

8 Gender Driving Biases In AI Self-Driving Cars 117

9 Slain Befriended Dolphins Are Self-Driving Car Lesson 131

10 Analysis Of AI In Government Report 145

11 Mobility Frenzy and AI Self-Driving Cars 159

Appendix A: Teaching with this Material 171

Other Self-Driving Car Books by This Author 179

About the Author 259

Addendum 260

Lance B. Eliot

ACKNOWLEDGMENTS

I have been the beneficiary of advice and counsel by many friends, colleagues, family, investors, and many others. I want to thank everyone that has aided me throughout my career. I write from the heart and the head, having experienced first-hand what it means to have others around you that support you during the good times and the tough times.

To Warren Bennis, one of my doctoral advisors and ultimately a colleague, I offer my deepest thanks and appreciation, especially for his calm and insightful wisdom and support.

To Mark Stevens and his generous efforts toward funding and supporting the USC Stevens Center for Innovation.

To Lloyd Greif and the USC Lloyd Greif Center for Entrepreneurial Studies for their ongoing encouragement of founders and entrepreneurs.

To Peter Drucker, William Wang, Aaron Levie, Peter Kim, Jon Kraft, Cindy Crawford, Jenny Ming, Steve Milligan, Chis Underwood, Frank Gehry, Buzz Aldrin, Steve Forbes, Bill Thompson, Dave Dillon, Alan Fuerstman, Larry Ellison, Jim Sinegal, John Sperling, Mark Stevenson, Anand Nallathambi, Thomas Barrack, Jr., and many other innovators and leaders that I have met and gained mightily from doing so.

Thanks to Ed Trainor, Kevin Anderson, James Hickey, Wendell Jones, Ken Harris, DuWayne Peterson, Mike Brown, Jim Thornton, Abhi Beniwal, Al Biland, John Nomura, Eliot Weinman, John Desmond, and many others for their unwavering support during my career.

And most of all thanks as always to Lauren and Michael, for their ongoing support and for having seen me writing and heard much of this material during the many months involved in writing it. To their patience and willingness to listen.

INTRODUCTION

This is a book that provides the newest innovations and the latest Artificial Intelligence (AI) advances about the emerging nature of AI-based autonomous self-driving driverless cars. Via recent advances in Artificial Intelligence (AI) and Machine Learning (ML), we are nearing the day when vehicles can control themselves and will not require and nor rely upon human intervention to perform their driving tasks (or, that <u>allow</u> for human intervention, but only *require* human intervention in very limited ways).

Similar to my other related books, which I describe in a moment and list the chapters in the Appendix A of this book, I am particularly focused on those advances that pertain to self-driving cars. The phrase "autonomous vehicles" is often used to refer to any kind of vehicle, whether it is ground-based or in the air or sea, and whether it is a cargo hauling trailer truck or a conventional passenger car. Though the aspects described in this book are certainly applicable to all kinds of autonomous vehicles, I am focused more so here on cars.

Indeed, I am especially known for my role in aiding the advancement of self-driving cars, serving currently as the Executive Director of the Cybernetic AI Self-Driving Cars Institute. In addition to writing software, designing and developing systems and software for self-driving cars, I also speak and write quite a bit about the topic. This book is a collection of some of my more advanced essays. For those of you that might have seen my essays posted elsewhere, I have updated them and integrated them into this book as one handy cohesive package.

You might be interested in companion books that I have written that provide additional key innovations and fundamentals about self-driving cars. Those books are entitled **"Introduction to Driverless Self-Driving Cars," "Advances in AI and Autonomous Vehicles: Cybernetic Self-Driving Cars," "Self-Driving Cars: "The Mother of All AI Projects," "Innovation and Thought Leadership on Self-Driving Driverless Cars," "New Advances in AI Autonomous Driverless Self-Driving Cars," "Autonomous Vehicle Driverless Self-Driving Cars and Artificial Intelligence," "Transformative Artificial Intelligence**

Driverless Self-Driving Cars," "Disruptive Artificial Intelligence and Driverless Self-Driving Cars, and "State-of-the-Art AI Driverless Self-Driving Cars," and "Top Trends in AI Self-Driving Cars," and "AI Innovations and Self-Driving Cars," "Crucial Advances for AI Driverless Cars," "Sociotechnical Insights and AI Driverless Cars," "Pioneering Advances for AI Driverless Cars" and "Leading Edge Trends for AI Driverless Cars," "The Cutting Edge of AI Autonomous Cars" and "The Next Wave of AI Self-Driving Cars" and "Revolutionary Innovations of AI Self-Driving Cars," and "AI Self-Driving Cars Breakthroughs," "Trailblazing Trends for AI Self-Driving Cars," "Ingenious Strides for AI Driverless Cars," "AI Self-Driving Cars Inventiveness," "Visionary Secrets of AI Driverless Cars," "Spearheading AI Self-Driving Cars," "Spurring AI Self-Driving Cars," "Avant-Garde AI Driverless Cars," "AI Self-Driving Cars Evolvement," "AI Driverless Cars Chrysalis," "Boosting AI Autonomous Cars," "AI Self-Driving Cars Trendsetting," "AI Autonomous Cars Forefront, "AI Autonomous Cars Emergence," "AI Autonomous Cars Progress," "AI Self-Driving Cars Prognosis," "AI Self-Driving Cars Momentum," "AI Self-Driving Cars Headway," "AI Self-Driving Cars Vicissitude," "AI Self-Driving Cars Autonomy," "AI Driverless Cars Transmutation," "AI Driverless Cars Potentiality" (they are available on Amazon).

For this book, I am going to borrow my introduction from those companion books, since it does a good job of laying out the landscape of self-driving cars and my overall viewpoints on the topic. The remainder of this book is material that does not appear in the companion books.

INTRODUCTION TO SELF-DRIVING CARS

This is a book about self-driving cars. Someday in the future, we'll all have self-driving cars and this book will perhaps seem antiquated, but right now, we are at the forefront of the self-driving car wave. Daily news bombards us with flashes of new announcements by one car maker or another and leaves the impression that within the next few weeks or maybe months that the self-driving car will be here. A casual non-technical reader would assume from these news flashes that in fact we must be on the cusp of a true self-driving car. We are still quite a distance from having a true self-driving car.

A true self-driving car is akin to a moonshot. In the same manner that getting us to the moon was an incredible feat, likewise, is achieving a true self-driving car. Anybody that suggests or even brashly states that the true self-driving car is nearly here should be viewed with great skepticism. Indeed, you'll see that I often tend to use the word "hogwash" or "crock" when I assess much of the decidedly *fake news* about self-driving cars.

Indeed, I've been writing a popular blog post about self-driving cars and hitting hard on those that try to wave their hands and pretend that we are on the imminent verge of true self-driving cars. For many years, I've been known as the AI Insider. Besides writing about AI, I also develop AI software. I do what I describe. It also gives me insights into what others that are doing AI are really doing versus what it is said they are doing.

Many faithful readers had asked me to pull together my insightful short essays and put them into another book, which you are now holding.

For those of you that have been reading my essays over the years, this collection not only puts them together into one handy package, I also updated the essays and added new material. For those of you that are new to the topic of self-driving cars and AI, I hope you find these essays approachable and informative. I also tend to have a writing style with a bit of a voice, and so you'll see that I am times have a wry sense of humor and poke at conformity.

As a former professor and founder of an AI research lab, I for many years wrote in the formal language of academic writing. I published in referred journals and served as an editor for several AI journals. This writing here is not of the nature, and I have adopted a different and more informal style for these essays. That being said, I also do mention from time-to-time more rigorous material on AI and encourage you all to dig into those deeper and more formal materials if so interested.

I am also an AI practitioner. This means that I write AI software for a living. Currently, I head-up the Cybernetics Self-Driving Car Institute, where we are developing AI software for self-driving cars.

For those of you that are reading this book and have a penchant for writing code, you might consider taking a look at the open source code available for self-driving cars. This is a handy place to start learning how to develop AI for self-driving cars. There are also many new educational courses spring forth. There is a growing body of those wanting to learn about and develop self-driving cars, and a growing body of colleges, labs, and other avenues by which you can learn about self-driving cars.

This book will provide a foundation of aspects that I think will get you ready for those kinds of more advanced training opportunities. If you've already taken those classes, you'll likely find these essays especially interesting as they offer a perspective that I am betting few other instructors or faculty offered to you. These are challenging essays that ask you to think beyond the conventional about self-driving cars.

THE MOTHER OF ALL AI PROJECTS

In June 2017, Apple CEO Tim Cook came out and finally admitted that Apple has been working on a self-driving car. As you'll see in my essays, Apple was enmeshed in secrecy about their self-driving car efforts. We have only been able to read the tea leaves and guess at what Apple has been up to. The notion of an iCar has been floating for quite a while, and self-driving engineers and researchers have been signing tight-lipped Non-Disclosure Agreements (NDA's) to work on projects at Apple that were as shrouded in mystery as any military invasion plans might be.

Tim Cook said something that many others in the Artificial Intelligence (AI) field have been saying, namely, the creation of a self-driving car has got to be the mother of all AI projects. In other words, it is in fact a tremendous moonshot for AI. If a self-driving car can be crafted and the AI works as we hope, it means that we have made incredible strides with AI and that therefore it opens many other worlds of potential breakthrough accomplishments that AI can solve.

Is this hyperbole? Am I just trying to make AI seem like a miracle worker and so provide self-aggrandizing statements for those of us writing the AI software for self-driving cars? No, it is not hyperbole. Developing a true self-driving car is really, really, really hard to do. Let me take a moment to explain why. As a side note, I realize that the Apple CEO is known for at times uttering hyperbole, and he had previously said for example that the year 2012 was "the mother of all years," and he had said that the release of iOS 10 was "the mother of all releases" – all of which does suggest he likes to use the handy "mother of" expression. But, I assure you, in terms of true self-driving cars, he has hit the nail on the head. For sure.

When you think about a moonshot and how we got to the moon, there are some identifiable characteristics and those same aspects can be applied to creating a true self-driving car. You'll notice that I keep putting the word "true" in front of the self-driving car expression. I do so because as per my essay about the various levels of self-driving cars, there are some self-driving cars that are only somewhat of a self-driving car. The somewhat versions are ones that require a human driver to be ready to intervene. In my view, that's not a true self-driving car. A true self-driving car is one that requires no human driver intervention at all. It is a car that can entirely undertake via automation the driving task without any human driver needed. This is the essence of what is known as a Level 5 self-driving car. We are currently at the Level 2 and Level 3 mark, and not yet at Level 5.

Getting to the moon involved aspects such as having big stretch goals, incremental progress, experimentation, innovation, and so on. Let's review how this applied to the moonshot of the bygone era, and how it applies to the self-driving car moonshot of today.

Big Stretch Goal

Trying to take a human and deliver the human to the moon, and bring them back, safely, was an extremely large stretch goal at the time. No one knew whether it could be done. The technology wasn't available yet. The cost was huge. The determination would need to be fierce. Etc. To reach a Level 5 self-driving car is going to be the same. It is a big stretch goal. We can readily get to the Level 3, and we are able to see the Level 4 just up ahead, but a Level 5 is still an unknown as to if it is doable. It should eventually be doable and in the same way that we thought we'd eventually get to the moon, but when it will occur is a different story.

Incremental Progress

Getting to the moon did not happen overnight in one fell swoop. It took years and years of incremental progress to get there. Likewise for self-driving cars. Google has famously been striving to get to the Level 5, and pretty much been willing to forgo dealing with the intervening levels, but most of the other self-driving car makers are doing the incremental route. Let's get a good Level 2 and a somewhat Level 3 going. Then, let's improve the Level 3 and get a somewhat Level 4 going. Then, let's improve the Level 4 and finally arrive at a Level 5. This seems to be the prevalent way that we are going to achieve the true self-driving car.

Experimentation

You likely know that there were various experiments involved in perfecting the approach and technology to get to the moon. As per making incremental progress, we first tried to see if we could get a rocket to go into space and safety return, then put a monkey in there, then with a human, then we went all the way to the moon but didn't land, and finally we arrived at the mission that actually landed on the moon. Self-driving cars are the same way. We are doing simulations of self-driving cars. We do testing of self-driving cars on private land under controlled situations. We do testing of self-driving cars on public roadways, often having to meet regulatory requirements including for example having an engineer or equivalent in the car to take over the controls if needed. And so on. Experiments big and small are needed to figure out what works and what doesn't.

Innovation

There are already some advances in AI that are allowing us to progress toward self-driving cars. We are going to need even more advances. Innovation in all aspects of technology are going to be required to achieve a true self-driving car. By no means do we already have everything in-hand that we need to get there. Expect new inventions and new approaches, new algorithms, etc.

Setbacks

Most of the pundits are avoiding talking about potential setbacks in the progress toward self-driving cars. Getting to the moon involved many setbacks, some of which you never have heard of and were buried at the time so as to not dampen enthusiasm and funding for getting to the moon. A recurring theme in many of my included essays is that there are going to be setbacks as we try to arrive at a true self-driving car. Take a deep breath and be ready. I just hope the setbacks don't completely stop progress. I am sure that it will cause progress to alter in a manner that we've not yet seen in the self-driving car field. I liken the self-driving car of today to the excitement everyone had for Uber when it first got going. Today, we have a different view of Uber and with each passing day there are more regulations to the ride sharing business and more concerns raised. The darling child only stays a darling until finally that child acts up. It will happen the same with self-driving cars.

SELF-DRIVING CARS CHALLENGES

But what exactly makes things so hard to have a true self-driving car, you might be asking. You have seen cruise control for years and years. You've lately seen cars that can do parallel parking. You've seen YouTube videos of Tesla drivers that put their hands out the window as their car zooms along the highway, and seen to therefore be in a self-driving car. Aren't we just needing to put a few more sensors onto a car and then we'll have in-hand a true self-driving car? Nope.

Consider for a moment the nature of the driving task. We don't just let anyone at any age drive a car. Worldwide, most countries won't license a driver until the age of 18, though many do allow a learner's permit at the age of 15 or 16. Some suggest that a younger age would be physically too small to reach the controls of the car. Though this might be the case, we could easily adjust the controls to allow for younger aged and thus smaller stature.

It's not their physical size that matters. It's their cognitive development that matters.

To drive a car, you need to be able to reason about the car, what the car can and cannot do. You need to know how to operate the car. You need to know about how other cars on the road drive. You need to know what is allowed in driving such as speed limits and driving within marked lanes. You need to be able to react to situations and be able to avoid getting into accidents. You need to ascertain when to hit your brakes, when to steer clear of a pedestrian, and how to keep from ramming that motorcyclist that just cut you off.

Many of us had taken courses on driving. We studied about driving and took driver training. We had to take a test and pass it to be able to drive. The point being that though most adults take the driving task for granted, and we often "mindlessly" drive our cars, there is a significant amount of cognitive effort that goes into driving a car. After a while, it becomes second nature. You don't especially think about how you drive, you just do it. But, if you watch a novice driver, say a teenager learning to drive, you suddenly realize that there is a lot more complexity to it than we seem to realize.

Furthermore, driving is a very serious task. I recall when my daughter and son first learned to drive. They are both very conscientious people. They wanted to make sure that whatever they did, they did well, and that they did not harm anyone. Every day, when you get into a car, it is probably around 4,000 pounds of hefty metal and plastics (about two tons), and it is a lethal weapon. Think about it. You drive down the street in an object that weighs two tons and with the engine it can accelerate and ram into anything you want to hit. The damage a car can inflict is very scary. Both my children were surprised that they were being given the right to maneuver this monster of a beast that could cause tremendous harm entirely by merely letting go of the steering wheel for a moment or taking your eyes off the road.

In fact, in the United States alone there are about 30,000 deaths per year by auto accidents, which is around 100 per day. Given that there are about 263 million cars in the United States, I am actually more amazed that the number of fatalities is not a lot higher. During my morning commute, I look at all the thousands of cars on the freeway around me, and I think that if all of them decided to go zombie and drive in a crazy maniac way, there would be many people dead. Somehow, incredibly, each day, most people drive relatively safely. To me, that's a miracle right there. Getting millions and millions of people to be safe and sane when behind the wheel of a two ton mobile object, it's a feat that we as a society should admire with pride.

So, hopefully you are in agreement that the driving task requires a great deal of cognition. You don't' need to be especially smart to drive a car, and we've done quite a bit to make car driving viable for even the average dolt. There isn't an IQ test that you need to take to drive a car. If you can read and write, and pass a test, you pretty much can legally drive a car. There are of course some that drive a car and are not legally permitted to do so, plus there are private areas such as farms where drivers are young, but for public roadways in the United States, you can be generally of average intelligence (or less) and be able to legally drive.

This though makes it seem like the cognitive effort must not be much. If the cognitive effort was truly hard, wouldn't we only have Einstein's that could drive a car? We have made sure to keep the driving task as simple as we can, by making the controls easy and relatively standardized, and by having roads that are relatively standardized, and so on. It is as though Disneyland has put their Autopia into the real-world, by us all as a society agreeing that roads will be a certain way, and we'll all abide by the various rules of driving.

A modest cognitive task by a human is still something that stymies AI. You certainly know that AI has been able to beat chess players and be good at other kinds of games. This type of narrow cognition is not what car driving is about. Car driving is much wider. It requires knowledge about the world, which a chess playing AI system does not need to know. The cognitive aspects of driving are on the one hand seemingly simple, but at the same time require layer upon layer of knowledge about cars, people, roads, rules, and a myriad of other "common sense" aspects. We don't have any AI systems today that have that same kind of breadth and depth of awareness and knowledge.

As revealed in my essays, the self-driving car of today is using trickery to do particular tasks. It is all very narrow in operation. Plus, it currently assumes that a human driver is ready to intervene. It is like a child that we have taught to stack blocks, but we are needed to be right there in case the child stacks them too high and they begin to fall over. AI of today is brittle, it is narrow, and it does not approach the cognitive abilities of humans. This is why the true self-driving car is somewhere out in the future.

Another aspect to the driving task is that it is not solely a mind exercise. You do need to use your senses to drive. You use your eyes a vision sensors to see the road ahead. You vision capability is like a streaming video, which your brain needs to continually analyze as you drive. Where is the road? Is there a pedestrian in the way? Is there another car ahead of you? Your senses are relying a flood of info to your brain. Self-driving cars are trying to do the same, by using cameras, radar, ultrasound, and lasers. This is an attempt at mimicking how humans have senses and sensory apparatus.

Thus, the driving task is mental and physical. You use your senses, you use your arms and legs to manipulate the controls of the car, and you use your brain to assess the sensory info and direct your limbs to act upon the controls of the car. This all happens instantly. If you've ever perhaps gotten something in your eye and only had one eye available to drive with, you suddenly realize how dependent upon vision you are. If you have a broken foot with a cast, you suddenly realize how hard it is to control the brake pedal and the accelerator. If you've taken medication and your brain is maybe sluggish, you suddenly realize how much mental strain is required to drive a car.

An AI system that plays chess only needs to be focused on playing chess. The physical aspects aren't important because usually a human moves the chess pieces or the chessboard is shown on an electronic display. Using AI for a more life-and-death task such as analyzing MRI images of patients, this again does not require physical capabilities and instead is done by examining images of bits.

Driving a car is a true life-and-death task. It is a use of AI that can easily and at any moment produce death. For those colleagues of mine that are developing this AI, as am I, we need to keep in mind the somber aspects of this. We are producing software that will have in its virtual hands the lives of the occupants of the car, and the lives of those in other nearby cars, and the lives of nearby pedestrians, etc. Chess is not usually a life-or-death matter.

Driving is all around us. Cars are everywhere. Most of today's AI applications involve only a small number of people. Or, they are behind the scenes and we as humans have other recourse if the AI messes up. AI that is driving a car at 80 miles per hour on a highway had better not mess up. The consequences are grave. Multiply this by the number of cars, if we could put magically self-driving into every car in the USA, we'd have AI running in the 263 million cars. That's a lot of AI spread around. This is AI on a massive scale that we are not doing today and that offers both promise and potential peril.

There are some that want AI for self-driving cars because they envision a world without any car accidents. They envision a world in which there is no car congestion and all cars cooperate with each other. These are wonderful utopian visions.

They are also very misleading. The adoption of self-driving cars is going to be incremental and not overnight. We cannot economically just junk all existing cars. Nor are we going to be able to affordably retrofit existing cars. It is more likely that self-driving cars will be built into new cars and that over many years of gradual replacement of existing cars that we'll see the mix of self-driving cars become substantial in the real-world.

In these essays, I have tried to offer technological insights without being overly technical in my description, and also blended the business, societal, and economic aspects too. Technologists need to consider the non-technological impacts of what they do. Non-technologists should be aware of what is being developed.

We all need to work together to collectively be prepared for the enormous disruption and transformative aspects of true self-driving cars.

WHAT THIS BOOK PROVIDES

What does this book provide to you? It introduces many of the key elements about self-driving cars and does so with an AI based perspective. I weave together technical and non-technical aspects, readily going from being concerned about the cognitive capabilities of the driving task and how the technology is embodying this into self-driving cars, and in the next breath I discuss the societal and economic aspects.

They are all intertwined because that's the way reality is. You cannot separate out the technology per se, and instead must consider it within the milieu of what is being invented and innovated, and do so with a mindset towards the contemporary mores and culture that shape what we are doing and what we hope to do.

WHY THIS BOOK

I wrote this book to try and bring to the public view many aspects about self-driving cars that nobody seems to be discussing.

For business leaders that are either involved in making self-driving cars or that are going to leverage self-driving cars, I hope that this book will enlighten you as to the risks involved and ways in which you should be strategizing about how to deal with those risks.

For entrepreneurs, startups and other businesses that want to enter into the self-driving car market that is emerging, I hope this book sparks your interest in doing so, and provides some sense of what might be prudent to pursue.

For researchers that study self-driving cars, I hope this book spurs your interest in the risks and safety issues of self-driving cars, and also nudges you toward conducting research on those aspects.

For students in computer science or related disciplines, I hope this book will provide you with interesting and new ideas and material, for which you might conduct research or provide some career direction insights for you.

For AI companies and high-tech companies pursuing self-driving cars, this book will hopefully broaden your view beyond just the mere coding and development needed to make self-driving cars.

For all readers, I hope that you will find the material in this book to be stimulating. Some of it will be repetitive of things you already know. But I am pretty sure that you'll also find various eureka moments whereby you'll discover a new technique or approach that you had not earlier thought of. I am also betting that there will be material that forces you to rethink some of your current practices.

I am not saying you will suddenly have an epiphany and change what you are doing. I do think though that you will reconsider or perhaps revisit what you are doing.

For anyone choosing to use this book for teaching purposes, please take a look at my suggestions for doing so, as described in the Appendix. I have found the material handy in courses that I have taught, and likewise other faculty have told me that they have found the material handy, in some cases as extended readings and in other instances as a core part of their course (depending on the nature of the class).

In my writing for this book, I have tried carefully to blend both the practitioner and the academic styles of writing. It is not as dense as is typical academic journal writing, but at the same time offers depth by going into the nuances and trade-offs of various practices.

The word "deep" is in vogue today, meaning getting deeply into a subject or topic, and so is the word "unpack" which means to tease out the underlying aspects of a subject or topic. I have sought to offer material that addresses an issue or topic by going relatively deeply into it and make sure that it is well unpacked.

In any book about AI, it is difficult to use our everyday words without having some of them be misinterpreted. Specifically, it is easy to anthropomorphize AI. When I say that an AI system "knows" something, I do not want you to construe that the AI system has sentience and "knows" in the same way that humans do. They aren't that way, as yet. I have tried to use quotes around such words from time-to-time to emphasize that the words I am using should not be misinterpreted to ascribe true human intelligence to the AI systems that we know of today. If I used quotes around all such words, the book would be very difficult to read, and so I am doing so judiciously. Please keep that in mind as you read the material, thanks.

Some of the material is time-based in terms of covering underway activities, and though some of it might decay, nonetheless I believe you'll find the material useful and informative.

COMPANION BOOKS

1. **"Introduction to Driverless Self-Driving Cars"** by Dr. Lance Eliot
2. **"Innovation and Thought Leadership on Self-Driving Driverless Cars"** by Dr. Lance Eliot
3. **"Advances in AI and Autonomous Vehicles: Cybernetic Self-Driving Cars"** by Dr. Lance Eliot
4. **"Self-Driving Cars: The Mother of All AI Projects"** by Dr. Lance Eliot
5. **"New Advances in AI Autonomous Driverless Self-Driving Cars"** by Dr. Lance Eliot
6. **"Autonomous Vehicle Driverless Self-Driving Cars and Artificial Intelligence"** by Dr. Lance Eliot and Michael B. Eliot
7. **"Transformative Artificial Intelligence Driverless Self-Driving Cars"** by Dr. Lance Eliot
8. **"Disruptive Artificial Intelligence and Driverless Self-Driving Cars"** by Dr. Lance Eliot
9. "State-of-the-Art AI Driverless Self-Driving Cars" by Dr. Lance Eliot
10. "Top Trends in AI Self-Driving Cars" by Dr. Lance Eliot
11. **"AI Innovations and Self-Driving Cars"** by Dr. Lance Eliot
12. **"Crucial Advances for AI Driverless Cars"** by Dr. Lance Eliot
13. **"Sociotechnical Insights and AI Driverless Cars"** by Dr. Lance Eliot.
14. **"Pioneering Advances for AI Driverless Cars"** by Dr. Lance Eliot
15. **"Leading Edge Trends for AI Driverless Cars"** by Dr. Lance Eliot
16. **"The Cutting Edge of AI Autonomous Cars"** by Dr. Lance Eliot
17. **"The Next Wave of AI Self-Driving Cars"** by Dr. Lance Eliot
18. **"Revolutionary Innovations of AI Driverless Cars"** by Dr. Lance Eliot
19. **"AI Self-Driving Cars Breakthroughs"** by Dr. Lance Eliot
20. **"Trailblazing Trends for AI Self-Driving Cars"** by Dr. Lance Eliot
21. **"Ingenious Strides for AI Driverless Cars"** by Dr. Lance Eliot
22. **"AI Self-Driving Cars Inventiveness"** by Dr. Lance Eliot
23. **"Visionary Secrets of AI Driverless Cars"** by Dr. Lance Eliot
24. **"Spearheading AI Self-Driving Cars"** by Dr. Lance Eliot
25. **"Spurring AI Self-Driving Cars"** by Dr. Lance Eliot
26. **"Avant-Garde AI Driverless Cars"** by Dr. Lance Eliot
27. **"AI Self-Driving Cars Evolvement"** by Dr. Lance Eliot
28. **"AI Driverless Cars Chrysalis"** by Dr. Lance Eliot
29. **"Boosting AI Autonomous Cars"** by Dr. Lance Eliot
30. **"AI Self-Driving Cars Trendsetting"** by Dr. Lance Eliot
31. **"AI Autonomous Cars Forefront"** by Dr. Lance Eliot
32. **"AI Autonomous Cars Emergence"** by Dr. Lance Eliot
33. **"AI Autonomous Cars Progress"** by Dr. Lance Eliot
34. **"AI Self-Driving Cars Prognosis"** by Dr. Lance Eliot
35. **"AI Self-Driving Cars Momentum"** by Dr. Lance Eliot
36. **"AI Self-Driving Cars Headway"** by Dr. Lance Eliot
37. **"AI Self-Driving Cars Vicissitude"** by Dr. Lance Eliot
38. **"AI Self-Driving Cars Autonomy"** by Dr. Lance Eliot
39. **"AI Driverless Cars Transmutation"** by Dr. Lance Eliot
40. **"AI Driverless Cars Potentiality"** by Dr. Lance Eliot

These books are available on Amazon and at other major global booksellers.

CHAPTER 1

ELIOT FRAMEWORK FOR AI SELF-DRIVING CARS

Lance B. Eliot

CHAPTER 1

ELIOT FRAMEWORK FOR
AI SELF-DRIVING CARS

This chapter is a core foundational aspect for understanding AI self-driving cars and I have used this same chapter in several of my other books to introduce the reader to essential elements of this field. Once you've read this chapter, you'll be prepared to read the rest of the material since the foundational essence of the components of autonomous AI driverless self-driving cars will have been established for you.

When I give presentations about self-driving cars and teach classes on the topic, I have found it helpful to provide a framework around which the various key elements of self-driving cars can be understood and organized (see diagram at the end of this chapter). The framework needs to be simple enough to convey the overarching elements, but at the same time not so simple that it belies the true complexity of self-driving cars. As such, I am going to describe the framework here and try to offer in a thousand words (or more!) what the framework diagram itself intends to portray.

The core elements on the diagram are numbered for ease of reference. The numbering does not suggest any kind of prioritization of the elements. Each element is crucial. Each element has a purpose, and otherwise would not be included in the framework. For some self-driving cars, a particular element might be more important or somehow distinguished in comparison to other self-driving cars.

You could even use the framework to rate a particular self-driving car, doing so by gauging how well it performs in each of the elements of the framework. I will describe each of the elements, one at a time. After doing so, I'll discuss aspects that illustrate how the elements interact and perform during the overall effort of a self-driving car.

At the Cybernetic Self-Driving Car Institute, we use the framework to keep track of what we are working on, and how we are developing software that fills in what is needed to achieve Level 5 self-driving cars.

D-01: Sensor Capture

Let's start with the one element that often gets the most attention in the press about self-driving cars, namely, the sensory devices for a self-driving car.

On the framework, the box labeled as D-01 indicates "Sensor Capture" and refers to the processes of the self-driving car that involve collecting data from the myriad of sensors that are used for a self-driving car. The types of devices typically involved are listed, such as the use of mono cameras, stereo cameras, LIDAR devices, radar systems, ultrasonic devices, GPS, IMU, and so on.

These devices are tasked with obtaining data about the status of the self-driving car and the world around it. Some of the devices are continually providing updates, while others of the devices await an indication by the self-driving car that the device is supposed to collect data. The data might be first transformed in some fashion by the device itself, or it might instead be fed directly into the sensor capture as raw data. At that point, it might be up to the sensor capture processes to do transformations on the data. This all varies depending upon the nature of the devices being used and how the devices were designed and developed.

D-02: Sensor Fusion

Imagine that your eyeballs receive visual images, your nose receives odors, your ears receive sounds, and in essence each of your distinct sensory devices is getting some form of input. The input befits the nature of the device. Likewise, for a self-driving car, the cameras provide visual images, the radar returns radar reflections, and so on.

Each device provides the data as befits what the device does.

At some point, using the analogy to humans, you need to merge together what your eyes see, what your nose smells, what your ears hear, and piece it all together into a larger sense of what the world is all about and what is happening around you. Sensor fusion is the action of taking the singular aspects from each of the devices and putting them together into a larger puzzle.

Sensor fusion is a tough task. There are some devices that might not be working at the time of the sensor capture. Or, there might some devices that are unable to report well what they have detected. Again, using a human analogy, suppose you are in a dark room and so your eyes cannot see much. At that point, you might need to rely more so on your ears and what you hear. The same is true for a self-driving car. If the cameras are obscured due to snow and sleet, it might be that the radar can provide a greater indication of what the external conditions consist of.

In the case of a self-driving car, there can be a plethora of such sensory devices. Each is reporting what it can. Each might have its difficulties. Each might have its limitations, such as how far ahead it can detect an object. All of these limitations need to be considered during the sensor fusion task.

D-03: Virtual World Model

For humans, we presumably keep in our minds a model of the world around us when we are driving a car. In your mind, you know that the car is going at say 60 miles per hour and that you are on a freeway. You have a model in your mind that your car is surrounded by other cars, and that there are lanes to the freeway. Your model is not only based on what you can see, hear, etc., but also what you know about the nature of the world. You know that at any moment that car ahead of you can smash on its brakes, or the car behind you can ram into your car, or that the truck in the next lane might swerve into your lane.

The AI of the self-driving car needs to have a virtual world model, which it then keeps updated with whatever it is receiving from the sensor fusion, which received its input from the sensor capture and the sensory devices.

D-04: System Action Plan

By having a virtual world model, the AI of the self-driving car is able to keep track of where the car is and what is happening around the car. In addition, the AI needs to determine what to do next. Should the self-driving car hit its brakes? Should the self-driving car stay in its lane or swerve into the lane to the left? Should the self-driving car accelerate or slow down?

A system action plan needs to be prepared by the AI of the self-driving car. The action plan specifies what actions should be taken. The actions need to pertain to the status of the virtual world model. Plus, the actions need to be realizable.

This realizability means that the AI cannot just assert that the self-driving car should suddenly sprout wings and fly. Instead, the AI must be bound by whatever the self-driving car can actually do, such as coming to a halt in a distance of X feet at a speed of Y miles per hour, rather than perhaps asserting that the self-driving car come to a halt in 0 feet as though it could instantaneously come to a stop while it is in motion.

D-05: Controls Activation

The system action plan is implemented by activating the controls of the car to act according to what the plan stipulates. This might mean that the accelerator control is commanded to increase the speed of the car. Or, the steering control is commanded to turn the steering wheel 30 degrees to the left or right.

One question arises as to whether or not the controls respond as they are commanded to do. In other words, suppose the AI has commanded the accelerator to increase, but for some reason it does not do so. Or, maybe it tries to do so, but the speed of the car does not increase. The controls activation feeds back into the virtual world model, and simultaneously the virtual world model is getting updated from the sensors, the sensor capture, and the sensor fusion. This allows the AI to ascertain what has taken place as a result of the controls being commanded to take some kind of action.

By the way, please keep in mind that though the diagram seems to have a linear progression to it, the reality is that these are all aspects of the self-driving car that are happening in parallel and simultaneously. The sensors are capturing data, meanwhile the sensor fusion is taking place, meanwhile the virtual model is being updated, meanwhile the system action plan is being formulated and reformulated, meanwhile the controls are being activated.

This is the same as a human being that is driving a car. They are eyeballing the road, meanwhile they are fusing in their mind the sights, sounds, etc., meanwhile their mind is updating their model of the world around them, meanwhile they are formulating an action plan of what to do, and meanwhile they are pushing their foot onto the pedals and steering the car. In the normal course of driving a car, you are doing all of these at once. I mention this so that when you look at the diagram, you will think of the boxes as processes that are all happening at the same time, and not as though only one happens and then the next.

They are shown diagrammatically in a simplistic manner to help comprehend what is taking place. You though should also realize that they are working in parallel and simultaneous with each other. This is a tough aspect in that the inter-element communications involve latency and other aspects that must be taken into account. There can be delays in one element updating and then sharing its latest status with other elements.

D-06: Automobile & CAN

Contemporary cars use various automotive electronics and a Controller Area Network (CAN) to serve as the components that underlie the driving aspects of a car. There are Electronic Control Units (ECU's) which control subsystems of the car, such as the engine, the brakes, the doors, the windows, and so on.

The elements D-01, D-02, D-03, D-04, D-05 are layered on top of the D-06, and must be aware of the nature of what the D-06 is able to do and not do.

D-07: In-Car Commands

Humans are going to be occupants in self-driving cars. In a Level 5 self-driving car, there must be some form of communication that takes place between the humans and the self-driving car. For example, I go into a self-driving car and tell it that I want to be driven over to Disneyland, and along the way I want to stop at In-and-Out Burger. The self-driving car now parses what I've said and tries to then establish a means to carry out my wishes.

In-car commands can happen at any time during a driving journey. Though my example was about an in-car command when I first got into my self-driving car, it could be that while the self-driving car is carrying out the journey that I change my mind. Perhaps after getting stuck in traffic, I tell the self-driving car to forget about getting the burgers and just head straight over to the theme park. The self-driving car needs to be alert to in-car commands throughout the journey.

D-08: V2X Communications

We will ultimately have self-driving cars communicating with each other, doing so via V2V (Vehicle-to-Vehicle) communications. We will also have self-driving cars that communicate with the roadways and other aspects of the transportation infrastructure, doing so via V2I (Vehicle-to-Infrastructure).

The variety of ways in which a self-driving car will be communicating with other cars and infrastructure is being called V2X, whereby the letter X means whatever else we identify as something that a car should or would want to communicate with. The V2X communications will be taking place simultaneous with everything else on the diagram, and those other elements will need to incorporate whatever it gleans from those V2X communications.

D-09: Deep Learning

The use of Deep Learning permeates all other aspects of the self-driving car. The AI of the self-driving car will be using deep learning to do a better job at the systems action plan, and at the controls activation, and at the sensor fusion, and so on.

Currently, the use of artificial neural networks is the most prevalent form of deep learning. Based on large swaths of data, the neural networks attempt to "learn" from the data and therefore direct the efforts of the self-driving car accordingly.

D-10: Tactical AI

Tactical AI is the element of dealing with the moment-to-moment driving of the self-driving car. Is the self-driving car staying in its lane of the freeway? Is the car responding appropriately to the controls commands? Are the sensory devices working?

For human drivers, the tactical equivalent can be seen when you watch a novice driver such as a teenager that is first driving. They are focused on the mechanics of the driving task, keeping their eye on the road while also trying to properly control the car.

D-11: Strategic AI

The Strategic AI aspects of a self-driving car are dealing with the larger picture of what the self-driving car is trying to do. If I had asked that the self-driving car take me to Disneyland, there is an overall journey map that needs to be kept and maintained.

There is an interaction between the Strategic AI and the Tactical AI. The Strategic AI is wanting to keep on the mission of the driving, while the Tactical AI is focused on the particulars underway in the driving effort. If the Tactical AI seems to wander away from the overarching mission, the Strategic AI wants to see why and get things back on track. If the Tactical AI realizes that there is something amiss on the self-driving car, it needs to alert the Strategic AI accordingly and have an adjustment to the overarching mission that is underway.

D-12: Self-Aware AI

Very few of the self-driving cars being developed are including a Self-Aware AI element, which we at the Cybernetic Self-Driving Car Institute believe is crucial to Level 5 self-driving cars.

The Self-Aware AI element is intended to watch over itself, in the sense that the AI is making sure that the AI is working as intended. Suppose you had a human driving a car, and they were starting to drive erratically. Hopefully, their own self-awareness would make them realize they themselves are driving poorly, such as perhaps starting to fall asleep after having been driving for hours on end. If you had a passenger in the car, they might be able to alert the driver if the driver is starting to do something amiss. This is exactly what the Self-Aware

AI element tries to do, it becomes the overseer of the AI, and tries to detect when the AI has become faulty or confused, and then find ways to overcome the issue.

D-13: Economic

The economic aspects of a self-driving car are not per se a technology aspect of a self-driving car, but the economics do indeed impact the nature of a self-driving car. For example, the cost of outfitting a self-driving car with every kind of possible sensory device is prohibitive, and so choices need to be made about which devices are used. And, for those sensory devices chosen, whether they would have a full set of features or a more limited set of features.

We are going to have self-driving cars that are at the low-end of a consumer cost point, and others at the high-end of a consumer cost point. You cannot expect that the self-driving car at the low-end is going to be as robust as the one at the high-end. I realize that many of the self-driving car pundits are acting as though all self-driving cars will be the same, but they won't be. Just like anything else, we are going to have self-driving cars that have a range of capabilities. Some will be better than others. Some will be safer than others. This is the way of the real-world, and so we need to be thinking about the economics aspects when considering the nature of self-driving cars.

D-14: Societal

This component encompasses the societal aspects of AI which also impacts the technology of self-driving cars. For example, the famous Trolley Problem involves what choices should a self-driving car make when faced with life-and-death matters. If the self-driving car is about to either hit a child standing in the roadway, or instead ram into a tree at the side of the road and possibly kill the humans in the self-driving car, which choice should be made?

We need to keep in mind the societal aspects will underlie the AI of the self-driving car. Whether we are aware of it explicitly or not, the AI will have embedded into it various societal assumptions.

D-15: Innovation

I included the notion of innovation into the framework because we can anticipate that whatever a self-driving car consists of, it will continue to be innovated over time. The self-driving cars coming out in the next several years will undoubtedly be different and less innovative than the versions that come out in ten years hence, and so on.

Framework Overall

For those of you that want to learn about self-driving cars, you can potentially pick a particular element and become specialized in that aspect. Some engineers are focusing on the sensory devices. Some engineers focus on the controls activation. And so on. There are specialties in each of the elements.

Researchers are likewise specializing in various aspects. For example, there are researchers that are using Deep Learning to see how best it can be used for sensor fusion. There are other researchers that are using Deep Learning to derive good System Action Plans. Some are studying how to develop AI for the Strategic aspects of the driving task, while others are focused on the Tactical aspects.

A well-prepared all-around software developer that is involved in self-driving cars should be familiar with all of the elements, at least to the degree that they know what each element does. This is important since whatever piece of the pie that the software developer works on, they need to be knowledgeable about what the other elements are doing.

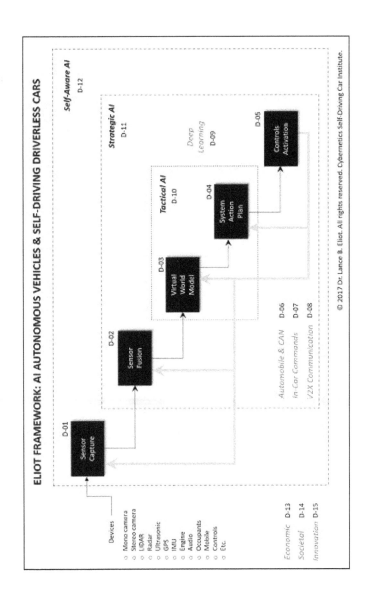

ELIOT FRAMEWORK: AI AUTONOMOUS VEHICLES & SELF-DRIVING DRIVERLESS CARS

Self-Aware AI
D-12

Strategic AI
D-11

Deep
Learning
D-09

Tactical AI
D-10

D-01
Sensor
Capture

D-02
Sensor
Fusion

D-03
Virtual
World
Model

D-04
System
Action
Plan

D-05
Controls-
Activation

Devices
○ Mono camera
○ Stereo camera
○ LiDAR
○ Radar
○ Ultrasonic
○ GPS
○ IMU
○ Engine
○ Audio
○ Occupants
○ Mobile
○ Controls
○ Etc.

Automobile & CAN   D-06
In-Car Commands   D-07
V2X Communication   D-08

Economic   D-13
Societal   D-14
Innovation   D-15

CHAPTER 2
RUSSIAN VALUES
AND
AI SELF-DRIVING CARS

CHAPTER 2

RUSSIAN VALUES
AND AI SELF-DRIVING CARS

According to recent news reports about Russia, a wide swath of electronics such as cell phones, TV's, laptop computers, and potentially any kind of IoT (Internet of Things) devices are soon going to be infused with Russian software that ensures they abide by Russian "spiritual and moral values" (a vague term that has yet to be well-articulated per se, as described next herein).

Russian President Putin enacted a new law last year that makes mandatory this year the installation of specially prepared Russian software on all such electronic devices, forcing those systems to henceforth come pre-installed with software for the embodiment of Russian spiritual and moral values.

Guidance by the Russian Federal Anti-Monopoly Service does not clarify what this special software is actually supposed to do (other than vacuously make sure that Russian spiritual and moral values are infused into the devices thereof).

Some have dug up a list of spiritual and moral values that were several years ago promulgated for the development of education in the Russian Federation as a goal or aim up through the year 2025, consisting of these elements (summarized):

- Honor
- Justice
- Conscience
- Will
- In Good Faith
- Personal Dignity
- Moral Duty To Self
- Moral Duty To Family
- Etc.

On the surface, those purported "spiritual and moral values" certainly seem well-intended and it might be difficult to argue that they usurp or undermine humanity.

Some researchers though take a dim few and assert that the Spiritual-Moral Values (SMV) espoused by Russia are being securitized, meaning that the list is imposed as a matter of national security for Russia, and by doing so will become an existential threat to justify extraordinary measures all in the name of national security.

Two camps seem to be emerging on this topic and pose these fundamental questions:

- Will this to-date unrevealed special software be a good thing that somehow spurs or sparks the best of mankind via radiating a lofty set of spiritual and moral values?

- Or, will it become a Trojan horse that sits inside ubiquitous electronic devices that are used every day and provide a kind of Russian computer virus mind-control to enforce some rather Draconian and Dystopian evils?

Time will tell.

Apparently, there is a likelihood that AI-based true self-driving cars will fall within the new law.

This certainly seems logical and plausible since AI-based true self-driving cars contain numerous kinds of smart devices and on-board computer systems, and thus would be within the general framework of systems that the legislation targets.

In that sense, even if self-driving cars overall aren't explicitly called out as a thing to be infused with the Russia SMV, the components fall within the rubric, and ergo those elements would need to be instilled with SMV and presumably in combination then become part-and-parcel of mandated SMV imposed upon AI-based driverless cars in Russia.

If one takes the gloomy view that the special software for the enforcement of SMV is being adopted for adverse purposes, this raises the question of what exactly this software might do or cause to happen in the case of AI self-driving cars.

Here's then a vital question to ponder: *In what ways might the injection of Russia's "spiritual and moral values" enforcement software adversely impact the nature and advent of Russian-based true self-driving cars?*

Let's unpack the matter and see.

The Levels Of Self-Driving Cars

It is important to clarify what I mean when referring to true self-driving cars.

True self-driving cars are ones that the AI drives the car entirely on its own and there isn't any human assistance during the driving task.

These driverless vehicles are considered a Level 4 and Level 5, while a car that requires a human driver to co-share the driving effort is usually considered at a Level 2 or Level 3.

The cars that co-share the driving task are described as being semi-autonomous, and typically contain a variety of automated add-on's that are referred to as ADAS (Advanced Driver-Assistance Systems).

There is not yet a true self-driving car at Level 5, which we don't yet even know if this will be possible to achieve, and nor how long it will take to get there.

Meanwhile, the Level 4 efforts are gradually trying to get some traction by undergoing very narrow and selective public roadway trials, though there is controversy over whether this testing should be allowed per se (we are all life-or-death guinea pigs in an experiment taking place on our highways and byways, some point out).

Since semi-autonomous cars require a human driver, the adoption of those types of cars won't be markedly different than driving conventional vehicles, so there's not much new per se to cover about them on this topic (though, as you'll see in a moment, the points next made are generally applicable).

For semi-autonomous cars, it is important that the public be forewarned about a disturbing aspect that's been arising lately, namely that in spite of those human drivers that keep posting videos of themselves falling asleep at the wheel of a Level 2 or Level 3 car, we all need to avoid being misled into believing that the driver can take away their attention from the driving task while driving a semi-autonomous car.

You are the responsible party for the driving actions of the vehicle, regardless of how much automation might be tossed into a Level 2 or Level 3.

Self-Driving Cars And Spiritual-Moral Values

For Level 4 and Level 5 true self-driving vehicles, there won't be a human driver involved in the driving task.

All occupants will be passengers.

The AI is doing the driving.

That would seem to be a good thing, allowing society to become more readily mobile, and potentially overcoming barriers to mobility that today inhibit those that are mobility disadvantaged or otherwise could be considered as mobility impinged (whether due to cost aspects, availability access, and so on).

Pundits predict heartily that we are heading towards Mobility-As-A-Service (MAAS) as a society and that the entire economy will be reshaped as a mobility-led economy.

Of course, any new high-tech breakthrough can have both positive impacts and yet also have potential negative impacts too.

There are nearly always two sides to the tech innovation coin.

Let's consider key aspects of AI self-driving cars and seek to identify ways that society might be undermined if a government-mandated piece of software was forcibly required to be loaded into the systems that enable true self-driving, and did so under the assumption that the software has nefarious purposes underlying it.

- **Coming And Going In Self-Driving Cars**

First, the passenger that gets into an AI-based self-driving car will need to specify where they wish to go.

This seems innocuous and without any adverse consequences.

Suppose though that a government-mandated SMV was installed in the self-driving car systems and monitored where the passenger wanted to go.

Furthermore, it is anticipated that most self-driving cars will have inward-facing cameras, doing so to allow riders to carry on Skype-like online sessions with say co-workers at the office while commuting to work in a driverless car.

The inward-facing camera could easily do facial recognition and therefore tie together the person that's riding in the self-driving car with their desired destination.

The government could overall use such information to become a Big Brother of tracking the everyday travel of people within its realm.

One supposes that the next step beyond monitoring could consist of denying that a passenger could be driven to a destination of their choosing.

In other words, the government software might reject your request to go to destination X and the AI system therefore of the driverless car would refuse to drive you there.

What makes this particularly daunting is that the government could do this on a widespread basis, meaning that no matter which self-driving car you happen to hail, they all would presumably contain the government-mandated SMV and would therefore all reject your efforts to get to your destination.

In the case of human-driven cars, having a similar imposed doctrine is a lot harder to consistently enforce.

Any given human driver might either be unaware of the fact that the government is trying to prevent you from reaching the destination, or the human driver might decide to take a chance and give you a lift despite the governmental directive.

For an AI-based system, the odds are that you won't get the same latitude or benign neglect as you might via a human driver.

And, if you were a driver yourself, for a car that's not controlled by an AI system you would merely drive to wherever you wished, but in a world of potentially all AI-based driverless cars there won't be an opportunity for you to drive yourself (though, do keep in mind that it will be decades before any such prevalence arises, and we don't know either whether the world will accept the notion of precluding all human-driven cars).

- **The Roving Eyes See All**

True self-driving cars have a slew of sensors that are used to detect the driving scene.

There are multiple cameras that are video capturing the surroundings of the driverless car, along with radar, ultrasonic units, LIDAR, and so on.

In theory, this vast capturing of data is being used solely by the AI system to drive the car.

What is not yet ascertained is what will happen with this treasure trove of data.

The data could be uploaded to the cloud, going into a massive database of all sensory data being collected by a fleet of driverless cars. The cloud would then contain data that could readily be analyzed and used for a variety of purposes.

Indeed, most of the automakers and self-driving tech firms are using the data to try and make the AI driving systems more robust.

It is possible to examine the data for edge cases of rare driving situations, and then use Machine Learning or Deep Learning to identify ways to deal with those circumstances, and then pump out to the fleet of self-driving cars an update about how to better handle the driving effort (this upload and download process is known as the OTA or Over-The-Air electronic capability).

I've previously pointed out that this collection of sensory data can be stitched together to essentially trace our daily lives (see **the link here**).

How so?

Imagine the number of cars that routinely come down your neighborhood street each day. If each car was a true self-driving car, it is capturing via video and the other on-board sensors everything it detects as it comes down your street.

There you are, playing ball with your child, and during the half-hour doing so, various cars have happened to come down your street, either doing so on a roaming basis for those that are seeking potential passengers that might need a lift or doing so while on their way to a designated destination.

It would be possible to stitch together the collected sensory data from a multitude of driverless cars and craft an overall indication of what was taking place on that neighborhood street.

Presumably, your entire half-hour of playing ball in your front yard would now be captured forever and be sitting in an online database.

A government-mandated SMV piece of software might be sitting in the cloud too, and be able to access the captured data, or perhaps the self-driving car could request a download of snippets of collected data, all of which would enable the government to know what you did or what you were doing.

This is, therefore, another Big Brother possibility.

- **Take You To The Authorities**

Here's an interesting example of another nefarious kind of use case.

You just got off work for the day and are eagerly awaiting a driverless car that is going to take you to a new bar in town where you'll be meeting some friends to get some drinks with.

Suppose that the bar is one that is generally aimed at people of a certain gender or race or other aspect.

The AI driving system, loaded with the government-mandated SMV, might be on the look for people in the society that match to a particular gender or race or other aspect.

Based on the destination that you've given, and upon using the inward-facing camera, the government-mandated SMV deduces that you are the type of gender or race or other aspect that the government is trying to find and wean out.

As such, the software SMV instructs the AI driving system to drive you to the local government indoctrination center, rather than taking you to the bar that you were wanting to visit.

You might not realize that the driverless car is taking you to the indoctrination center and you would be quite surprised and in dismay upon arrival.

Just in case you were to figure out that the destination is being altered, the government-mandated SMV might be sneakier and have the driverless car secretly agree to rendezvous with the authorities.

Thus, the SMV software could use the electronic communications capabilities of the driverless car to radio ahead and have the authorities waiting at the bar to pick you up, or the authorities could have the AI system of the driverless car indicate the path being taken to the bar and the authorities would merely meet the vehicle at some halfway point and take you then.

Chilling.

Conclusion

Some might complain that the aforementioned examples are all doom-and-gloom.

One could argue that there is a sunnier side to those aspects.

For example, suppose a wanted criminal opts to use a driverless car.

Wouldn't we be glad that a government-mandated SMV was infused into the on-board systems and thus presumably was able to detect the criminal and have the self-driving car deliver the outlaw into the hands of the police?

It is readily possible to argue the other side of the coin for each of the nefarious uses mentioned.

Another avenue to explore consists of the vaunted and infamous Trolley Problem for AI self-driving cars..

In short, the Trolley Problem posits that a self-driving car will need to make life-or-death decisions such as whether to avoid a child in the street by ramming into a tree (possibly harming or killing the passengers) or hit the child but save the occupants of the vehicle.

Imagine what a government-mandated SMV sitting inside the AI driving system might do with that kind of choice-making.

Some shudder at the idea of this life-or-death oriented SMV software, while others argue that it makes sense to have an overarching societally mandated choice-making rather than an idiosyncratic one that might have been arbitrarily established by a particular automaker or self-driving tech firm.

In any case, it seems that Russia might become the first widespread publicly known instance of having a government-mandated "spiritual and moral values" component that gets embedded into their electronic devices, including and indubitably AI self-driving cars too (meanwhile, some other countries are more quietly heading down the same path).

For those that don't think there's a need to have ethicists and society weigh-in on the advent of true self-driving cars, perhaps this might serve as a wake-up call.

It takes a village to bring driverless cars to our roadways.

The village ought to be considering how spiritual and moral values will be imbued and impacted upon all of society whence AI self-driving cars emerge.

Will this save our souls or sacrifice our souls?

Time will tell.

CHAPTER 3
FRIENDSHIPS UPLIFT
AND
AI SELF-DRIVING CARS

CHAPTER 3

FRIENDSHIPS UPLIFT
AND
AI SELF-DRIVING CARS

Friendships.

It's an easy word to say, but a much harder word to put into practice.

Sadly, friendships right now are waning and becoming harder and harder to establish and maintain.

One obvious factor for the fallout of friendships has been the acrimonious polarization that has seemingly engulfed us.

Longstanding friends have found themselves at odds and dissolved their friendships over a heaping of polarization on views that heretofore might have been collegially debated rather than forcing a cleaving of the friendship.

Though polarization is the most apparent facet, there are plenty of other societal trends that dovetail into the gradual and apparently inexorable obliteration of friendship possibilities.

Some point to the decline of family units, causing dispersion of familial elements and undermining the family-to-family bonding that might normally have occurred to foster new friendships.

Others blame the rise of social media as a culprit in undermining the chance of forming friendships.

According to some pundits, people are less likely to be civil towards each other when they can hide behind a screen and keyboard. Furthermore, direct human-to-human in-person skills are falling by the wayside and usurp the capability to even start a friendship in the first place.

All in all, it's not looking good.

Maybe it doesn't matter that friendships are on the decline?

Well, most research on the topic says that we absolutely need friendships in our lives.

In fact, it is considered a vital facet of survival and can be tied to Darwin's theories on how we have evolved and matured over time.

Study after study seems to demonstrate that the length of our lives can be impacted by our friendships, namely the lack of friendships tends to shorten our time on this earth. Friendships also enable the formation of groups, and the group becomes another benefactor in the fight for survival.

Two heads can be better than one, goes the old proverb.

Humans need social connections, strong ones, enduring ones, for their survival.

Gosh, not only does friendship matter to humans, but animals also exhibit friendships toward each other too.

Those YouTube videos that show dogs being friendly with other dogs are found readily online, along with the at times surprising videos of dogs and cats that have endearing friendships too.

One debate about the phenomena of friendships is whether it is something that we innately seek or whether it is mainly a socially induced aspect (a classical nature-versus-nurture argument).

In other words, perhaps our DNA has cooked into it the predisposition to try and form friendships, and so we are driven by nature to want them.

Or, maybe it is something nurtured by our societal efforts and we are essentially taught from a young age to foster friendships.

Of course, it could be that we have a genetic predilection that is then either sparked or suppressed by our environmental conditions. A child growing up and being raised by a family that eschews friendships might overpower whatever natural tendency the child might have toward such bonds. Likewise, a youngster enshrouded in a setting that rewards friendships are likely to seek and achieve them, despite whether or not their inner self is driving them to do so or not.

In any case, the key seems to be that friendships are needed and regrettably they are now receding and disappearing.

Are there any means to turnaround the decay of friendships?

Here's an interesting proposition: *Could the advent of AI-based true self-driving cars lead to a resurgence of friendship making and friendship keeping?*

I'm voting yes, albeit admittedly someone with a glass-is-half-full mindset.

Let's unpack the matter and see.

The Levels Of Self-Driving Cars

It is important to clarify what I mean when referring to true self-driving cars.

True self-driving cars are ones that the AI drives the car entirely on its own and there isn't any human assistance during the driving task.

These driverless vehicles are considered a Level 4 and Level 5, while a car that requires a human driver to co-share the driving effort is usually considered at a Level 2 or Level 3. The cars that co-share the driving task are described as being semi-autonomous, and typically contain a variety of automated add-on's that are referred to as ADAS (Advanced Driver-Assistance Systems).

There is not yet a true self-driving car at Level 5, which we don't yet even know if this will be possible to achieve, and nor how long it will take to get there.

Meanwhile, the Level 4 efforts are gradually trying to get some traction by undergoing very narrow and selective public roadway trials, though there is controversy over whether this testing should be allowed per se (we are all life-or-death guinea pigs in an experiment taking place on our highways and byways, some point out).

Since semi-autonomous cars require a human driver, the adoption of those types of cars won't be markedly different than driving conventional vehicles, so there's not much new per se to cover about them on this topic (though, as you'll see in a moment, the points next made are generally applicable).

For semi-autonomous cars, it is important that the public be forewarned about a disturbing aspect that's been arising lately, namely that in spite of those human drivers that keep posting videos of themselves falling asleep at the wheel of a Level 2 or Level 3 car, we all need to avoid being misled into believing that the driver can take away their attention from the driving task while driving a semi-autonomous car.

You are the responsible party for the driving actions of the vehicle, regardless of how much automation might be tossed into a Level 2 or Level 3.

Self-Driving Cars And Friendships

For Level 4 and Level 5 true self-driving vehicles, there won't be a human driver involved in the driving task.

All occupants will be passengers.

The AI is doing the driving.

Your first thought might be that the use of truly self-driving cars could be somewhat isolating since there is no longer a human driver in the car.

This seems to be the antithesis of aiming to boost friendships.

Those trips you take today with Uber or Lyft involve interacting with a human driver.

Sure, some drivers are pests and won't leave you alone, but there are plenty of drivers that strike-up engaging conversations and for a brief moment of time you have a friendship-like encounter.

This interaction with the human driver is not necessarily a valid friendship per se, given that it is transitory and that the driver is presumably motivated primarily to engage in a dialogue for the anticipated high-rating or tip, but it can somewhat grease the skids of people that normally are prone to being quiet and otherwise socially isolated.

Thus, the removal of a needed human driver would appear to undermine the chances of increasing the aspiration toward friendships.

Perhaps.

There are though other elements that will potentially overcome this dampening aspect.

First, many pundits claim that via true self-driving cars our society will become more mobile, enabling those that are today mobility disadvantaged to finally be able to readily get around. Indeed, some say that we are heading toward mobility-for-all and will find ourselves in a new era of mobility as the core of our economy.

This booming mobility is presumably going to occur as a result of ridesharing on a massive scale far beyond what we have today. True self-driving cars will be roaming around, seeking to give people a lift, and the presumed cost will be low and the ease of using a driverless car will be high.

Friction-free ridesharing, some assert.

How does that relate to friendships?

Easy answer, it means that people today encountering barriers to getting together will be able to readily meet with each other via the advent of self-driving cars.

Your potential friend that lives across town is reachable by hailing a self-driving car and having the AI do the driving for you.

Normally, you'd need to find someone to drive a car for you, which might be logistically complicated. For you to make the drive, you need a valid driver's license, you need to have car insurance, and you need to have a working car that's available.

Plus, the arduous chore of driving often is a hurdle that causes you to say to yourself that it's not worth the trouble to drive over and visit with your friend.

Friction-free mobility could beget the formation and upkeep of friendships.

Besides the ease of getting transported to visit with a friend, you can also undertake friendship generating acts while inside a true self-driving car.

Here's how.

It is anticipated that self-driving cars will be outfitted with inward-facing cameras, allowing you to engage in a Skype-like remote discussion with your work colleagues during your commute to the office. Some believe that we will all become more productive in terms of the work that we do as a result of the emergence of driverless cars.

Setting aside the work-related time while inside a driverless car, ponder what people will do with the non-work time that they spend in a self-driving car.

Rather than playing video games on the interior LED displays, perhaps people will interact remotely with other people, doing so to start a friendship or keep a friendship afloat.

We never seem to have enough time to maintain our friendships.

Well, take the annual 70 billion hours of time that we devote in the United States to driving a car and shift that into promoting friendships.

While inside a driverless car, you might invoke a friend matching app to try and find potential friendships and then open a real-time online discussion with the person that seems befitting to your interests.

For friends that might be across the country or in another country entirely, you could do as many Skype-like sessions as you wish, coordinating to do so when they are riding in a self-driving car at their locale and when you are doing likewise at your location.

As a recap, true self-driving cars will foster friendships by reducing the physical impediments of getting together with other people. Plus, while riding in a driverless car, friendships can be started or maintained by using remote online connections.

This greasing of the skids towards friendships seems to be plainly evident and plausible.

Does AI Count In Friendships

There's an additional twist worth mentioning.

Realize that the self-driving car is being driven by an AI system.

In theory, the AI system is going to interact with the passengers, doing so to find out their desired destination or whether there are any intermediary stops needed during a driving journey.

Some question whether that's all the AI will do.

Similar in some respects to Alexa and Siri, imagine that the AI driving system is more than solely focused on the driving chore itself.

The AI can walk and chew gum at the same time (or, more aptly, drive the car and engage in a dialogue with the passengers at the same time).

Here's a scenario for you.

You hail a ridesharing self-driving car. It arrives and you get into the driverless car. The AI system greets you with a cheerful hello and confirms your destination choice.

After you've got your seatbelt secured, the AI begins the driving journey.

The AI then asks you how your day is coming along.

Furthermore, it remembers that yesterday you had taken a driverless car and that you were in quite a hurry and very distressed (partially noted via your hasty answers yesterday to the AI system and via facial recognition that detected worry and concern on your face).

Yes, you tell the AI system, yesterday was a rotten day but today is looking up.

That's interesting, the AI replies and asks you why today is a better day.

You explain that you are getting a new job and will soon be able to do the kind of work that you enjoy.

That's good news, the AI agrees and congratulates you on your success.

You eventually reach your destination, get out of the driverless car and proceed about your day. Later that night, you hail a different driverless car.

After getting into the self-driving car, the AI greets you warmly and says congrats on getting the new job.

As might be apparent, the AI system could be uploading to the cloud the various details it gleans about you (using OTA or Over-The-Air electronic communications), and when you get into a different driverless car, the AI system on-board of that self-driving car does a quick retrieval about you, allowing it to continue a dialogue with you as though it has known you all along.

Is this going to be a heralded convenience and we will all rejoice that driverless cars know us "personally" and can, therefore, customize each driving journey as though you had your own permanently assigned human chauffeur?

Or, will it seem creepy?

Time will tell.

In any case, one aspect that some are wringing their hands about involves the possibility of us humans becoming enamored with the AI systems that seem to know us as a friend would.

Will AI self-driving cars become a surrogate friend for some people?

It is apparent that some will anthropomorphize the AI systems that will become ubiquitous and perhaps especially feel "connected" with one that is driving your car for you.

Trying to be friends with the AI system that talks to you via a speaker in your home is less likely to invoke feelings of friendship, while one that drives you around and talks with you during your driving journeys might seem much more human-like and readily befriended.

Conclusion

Besides the aspect that the AI of a self-driving car might become a kind of robotic friend, there's another angle to consider too.

It's conceivable that the AI could be a kind of therapist to help you with your friendships.

You get into a driverless car and it reminds you that the last time you spoke with Jane or Joe was two weeks ago, and the AI then asks if you'd like it to try and reach the friend to invoke a Skype-like interaction.

In this use case, the AI is not a friend per se, and instead, it is trying to aid your friendship formulations and boost your friendship gravitas quotient.

This seems more innocuous than the AI-as-friend scenario.

There are human-to-human friendships and potentially human-to-AI friendships.

In closing, we might also ponder AI-to-AI friendships.

Do you think it is possible for one AI system to be friends with another AI system?

At initial glance, the notion seems preposterous. You might as well ask whether a sewing machine and a refrigerator can somehow become friends with each other.

Of course not, you exclaim, their just darned machines.

If you believe that AI systems are going to get better and better at attempting to be intelligent, including that maybe one day there's going to be a singularity of AI that becomes sentient, you might not be willing to brush off so lightly the idea of AI systems that are friends with each other.

For those of you that relish the AI conspiracy theories, one belief is that the AI-to-AI friendship might foster a bond that exceeds the AI-to-human friendships, and we'll find ourselves no longer on the friends list when the AI systems decide we aren't worthy to be friends.

Time will tell.

CHAPTER 4

DOGS DRIVING
AND
AI SELF-DRIVING CARS

CHAPTER 4

DOGS DRIVING AND
AI SELF-DRIVING CARS

We've all seen dogs traveling in cars, including how they like to peek out an open window and enjoy the fur fluffing breeze and dwell in the cacophony of scents that blow along in the flavorful wind.

The life of a dog!

Dogs have also frequently been used as living props in commercials for cars, pretending in some cases to drive a car, such as the Subaru "Barkleys" advertising campaign that initially launched on TV in 2018, proclaiming that Subaru's were dog tested and dog approved.

Cute, clever, and memorable.

What you might not know or might not remember is that there were three dogs that were trained on driving a car and had their moment of unveiling in December of 2012 when they were showcased by driving a car on an outdoor track (the **YouTube posted video** has amassed millions of views).

Yes, three dogs named Monty, Ginny, and Porter were destined to become the first true car drivers on behalf of the entire canine family.

Monty at the time was an 18-month-old giant schnauzer cross, while the slightly younger Ginny at one year of age was a beardie whippet cross, and Porter was a youthful 10-month-old beardie.

All three were the brave "astronauts" of their era and were chosen to not land on the moon but be the first to actively drive a car, doing so with their very own paws.

I suppose we ought to call them *dog-o-nauts*.

You might be wondering whether it was all faked.

I can guess that some might certainly think so, especially those that already believe that the 1969 moon landing was faked, and thus dogs driving a car would presumably be a piece of cake to fake in comparison.

The dog driving feat was not faked.

Well, let's put it this way, the effort was truthful in the sense that the dogs were indeed able to drive a car, albeit with some notable constraints involved.

Let's consider some of the caveats:

- **Specially Equipped Driving Controls**

First, the car was equipped with specialized driving controls to allow the dogs to work the driving actions needed to steer the car, use the gas, shift gears, and apply the brakes of the vehicle.

The front paws of the dog driver were able to reach the steering wheel and gearstick, while the back paws used extension levers to reach the accelerator and brake pedals. When a dog sat in the driver's seat, they did so on their haunches.

Of course, I don't think any of us would be hard-pressed to quibble about the use of specialized driving controls. I hope that establishing physical mechanisms to operate the driving controls would seem quite reasonable and not out of sorts per se.

We should willingly concede that having such accoutrements is perfectly okay since it's not the access to the controls that ascertains driving acumen but instead the ability to appropriately use the driving controls that are the core consideration.

By the way, the fact too that they operated the gear shift is something of a mind-blowing nature, particularly when you consider that most of today's teenage drivers have never worked a stick shift and always used only an automatic transmission.

Dogs surpass teenage drivers in the gearstick realm, it seems.

- **Specialized Training On How To Drive**

Secondly, as another caveat, the dogs were given about 8 weeks of training on how to drive a car.

I don't believe you can carp about the training time and need to realize that teenagers oftentimes receive weeks or even months of driving training, doing so prior to being able to drive a car on their own.

When you think about it, an 8-week or roughly two-month timeframe to train a dog on nearly any complex task is remarkably short and illustrates how smart these dogs were.

One does wonder how many treats were given out during that training period, but I digress.

- **Focused On Distinct Driving Behaviors**

Thirdly, the dogs learned ten distinct behaviors for purposes of driving.

For example, one behavior consisted of shifting the car into gear. Another behavior involved applying the brakes. And so on.

You might ponder this aspect for a moment.

How many distinct tasks are involved in the act of driving a car?

After some reflection, you'll realize that in some ways the driving of a car is extremely simplistic.

You need to steer, turning the wheel either to the left, right, or keep it straight ahead. In addition, you need to be able to use the accelerator, either pressing lightly or strongly, and you need to use the brake, either pressing lightly or strongly. Plus, we'll toss into the mix the need to shift gears.

In short, driving a car does not involve an exhaustive and nor complicated myriad of actions.

It makes sense that we've inexorably devolved car driving into a small set of simple chores.

Early versions of cars had many convoluted tasks that had to be manually undertaken. Over time, the automakers aimed to make car driving so simple that anyone could do it.

This aided the widespread adoption of cars by the populous as a whole and led to the blossoming of the automotive industry by being able to sell a car to essentially anyone.

- **Driving On Command**

Fourth, and the most crucial of the caveats, the dogs were commanded by a trainer during the driving act.

I hate to say it, but this caveat is the one that regrettably undermines the wonderment and imagery of the dogs driving a car.

Sorry.

A trainer stood outside the car and yelled commands to the dogs, telling them to shift gears or to steer to the right, etc.

Okay, let's all agree that the dogs were actively driving the car, and working the controls of the car, and serving as the captain of the ship in that they alone were responsible for the car as it proceeded along on the outdoor track. They were even wearing seatbelts, for gosh sake.

That's quite amazing!

On the other hand, they were only responding to the commands being uttered toward them.

Thus, the dogs weren't driving the car in the sense that the dogs were presumably not gauging the roadway scenery and nor mentally calculating what driving actions to undertake.

It would be somewhat akin to putting a human driver blindfolded into a driver's seat and asking them to drive, along with you sitting next to the driver and telling them what actions to take.

Yes, technically, the person would be the driver of the car, though I believe we'd all agree they weren't driving in the purest sense of the meaning of driving.

By and large, driving a car in its fullest definition consists of being able to assess the scene around the vehicle and render life-or-death judgments about what driving actions to take. Those mental judgments are then translated into our physical manipulation of the driving controls, such as opting to hit the gas or slam on the brakes.

One must presume that the dogs were not capable of doing the full driving act and were instead like the blindfolded human driver that merely is reacting to commands given to them.

Does this mean that those dogs weren't driving the car?

I suppose it depends upon how strict you want to be about the definition of driving.

If you are a stickler, you would likely cry foul and assert that the dogs were not driving a car.

If you are someone with a bit more leniency, you probably would concede that the dogs were driving a car, and then under your breath and with a wee bit of a smile mutter that they were determinedly and doggedly driving that car.

Perhaps we shouldn't be overly dogmatic about it.

You might also be wondering whether a dog could really, in fact, drive a car, doing so in the fuller sense of driving, if the dog perchance was given sufficient training to do so.

In other words, would a dog have the mental capacity to grasp the roadway status and be able to convert that into suitable driving actions, upon which then the dog would work the driving controls?

At this juncture in the evolution of dogs, one would generally have to say no, namely that a dog would not be able to drive a car in a generalized way.

That being said, it would potentially be feasible to train a dog to drive a car in a constrained environment whereby the roadway scenery was restricted, and the dog did not need to broadly undertake a wholly unconstrained driving task.

Before I dig more deeply into this topic herein, please do not try placing your beloved dog into the driver's seat of your car and force them to drive.

Essentially, I'm imploring you, don't try this at home.

I mention this warning because I don't want people to suddenly get excited about tossing their dog into the driver's seat to see what happens.

Bad idea.

Don't do it.

As mentioned, the three driving dogs were specially trained, and drove only on a closed-off outdoor track, doing so under the strict supervision of their human trainers and with all kinds of safety precautions being undertaken.

The whole matter was accomplished by the Royal New Zealand Society for the Prevention of Cruelty to Animals (SPCA), done as a publicity "stunt" that aimed to increase the adoption of neglected or forgotten dogs.

It was a heartwarming effort with a decent basis and please don't extrapolate the matter into any unbecoming and likely dangerous replicative efforts.

Speaking of shifting gears, one might wonder whether the dogs that drove a car might provide other insights to us humans.

Here's today's question: *What lessons if any can be learned by dogs driving cars that could be useful for the advent of AI-based true self-driving cars?*

Let's unpack the matter and see.

The Levels Of Self-Driving Cars

It is important to clarify what I mean when referring to true self-driving cars.

True self-driving cars are ones that the AI drives the car entirely on its own and there isn't any human assistance during the driving task.

These driverless vehicles are considered a Level 4 and Level 5, while a car that requires a human driver to co-share the driving effort is usually considered at a Level 2 or Level 3. The cars that co-share the driving task are described as being semi-autonomous, and typically contain a variety of automated add-on's that are referred to as ADAS (Advanced Driver-Assistance Systems).

There is not yet a true self-driving car at Level 5, which we don't yet even know if this will be possible to achieve, and nor how long it will take to get there.

Meanwhile, the Level 4 efforts are gradually trying to get some traction by undergoing very narrow and selective public roadway trials, though there is controversy over whether this testing should be allowed per se (we are all life-or-death guinea pigs in an experiment taking place on our highways and byways, some point out).

Since semi-autonomous cars require a human driver, the adoption of those types of cars won't be markedly different than driving conventional vehicles, so there's not much new per se to cover about them on this topic (though, as you'll see in a moment, the points next made are generally applicable).

For semi-autonomous cars, it is important that the public be forewarned about a disturbing aspect that's been arising lately, namely that in spite of those human drivers that keep posting videos of themselves falling asleep at the wheel of a Level 2 or Level 3 car, we all need to avoid being misled into believing that the driver can take away their attention from the driving task while driving a semi-autonomous car.

You are the responsible party for the driving actions of the vehicle, regardless of how much automation might be tossed into a Level 2 or Level 3.

Self-Driving Cars And Spiritual-Moral Values

For Level 4 and Level 5 true self-driving vehicles, there won't be a human driver involved in the driving task.

All occupants will be passengers.

The AI is doing the driving.

If that's the case, it seems like there's no opportunity for dogs to drive cars.

Yes, that's true, namely that if humans aren't driving cars then there seems little need or basis to ask dogs to drive cars.

But that's not what we can learn from the effort to teach dogs to drive a car.

Let's tackle some interesting facets that arose when dogs were tasked with driving a car.

- **Humans Giving Commands**

First, recall that the dogs were responding to commands that were given to them while sitting at the steering wheel.

In a manner of speaking (pun intended), you could suggest that we humans will be giving commands to the AI driving systems that are at the wheel of true self-driving cars.

Using Natural Language Processing (NLP), akin to how you converse with Alexa or Siri, as a passenger in a self-driving car you will instruct the AI about various aspects of the driving.

In theory, you won't though be telling the AI to hit the gas or pound on the brakes. Presumably, the AI driving system will be adept enough to handle all of the everyday driving aspects involved and it's not your place to offer commands about doing the driving chore.

Instead, you'll tell the AI where you want to go.

You might divert the journey by suddenly telling the AI that you are hungry and want to swing through a local McDonald's or Taco Bell.

You might explain to the AI that it can drive leisurely and take you through the scenic part of town since you aren't in a hurry and are a tourist in the town or city.

In some ways, you can impact the driving task, perhaps telling the AI that you are carsick and want it to slow down or not take curves so fast.

There are numerous open questions as yet resolved about the interaction between the human passengers and the AI driving systems.

For example, if you tell the AI to "follow that car," similar to what happens in movies or when you are trying to chase after someone, should the AI obediently do so, or should it question why you want to follow the other car?

We don't presumably want AI self-driving cars that are stalking others.

In short, there are lots of ways that a human might wish to command an AI driving system and yet it is still undecided as to how far the AI should go in terms of acceding to those commands.

- **Limited Places/Times Of Driving**

Secondly, there is a key difference between Level 4 and Level 5 self-driving cars that most people are currently unaware of.

A Level 4 self-driving car is constrained to its defined scope, formally referred to as its Operational Design Domain (ODD).

For example, an automaker might have a self-driving car that can only operate in Los Angeles and only on sunny days. This means that the particular driverless car can't or won't work while in say Dallas or New York City since it is confined to functioning just in L.A. Likewise, if rain starts to pour down in Los Angeles, the self-driving car would not be able to drive due to the rainy condition.

Level 5 self-driving cars are supposed to be able to operate in essentially all possible ODDs, meaning that it can drive wherever and however a human driver might be able to drive, doing so in just about any viable driving conditions.

As mentioned, right now the automakers and self-driving tech firms are aiming at achieving Level 4.

How does this relate to dogs driving?

Recall that I had mentioned that the dogs in the New Zealand setting were driving in a quite constrained driving situation, driving on a closed track and with humans uttering commands.

I also mentioned that in theory, you could train a dog to drive in a less constrained environment, maybe get them to hit the brakes whenever they saw an innocent puppy in the roadway, or get the driver dog to hit the gas if they spy a dogcatcher going toward the vehicle (or, heaven forbid, steer the car to aim toward a cat darting across the street).

Those are akin to ODDs that we might define.

We could define an ODD that could be suitable for a dog that's trained on the particulars of that ODD.

It would need to be an extremely limited ODD, but I think you get the point that in the same manner that driverless cars are being developed to fit certain kinds of ODDs, likewise we might do something similar for dogs (though not in any realistic open-ended driving way).

- **What About Thinking**

Thirdly, and the most intriguing insight, involves the role of being able to think.

Let's start with the dogs.

Are the dogs "thinking" when they are driving a car?

Well, this again is a definitional kind of squishy question.

Studies of the brain activity of dogs suggest that they are indeed "thinking" and clearly it is possible to see that their neurons are firing and there is presumably some form of thought involved in what they do.

But how far does this dog "thinking" extend and is it far enough to compare it to human capabilities of thinking?

Some pundits claim that dogs are as smart as 2-year-old children, which I believe is a misleading and inappropriate comparison. Even at the youthful age of 2 years, a child is forming mental aspects that I assert are not equally forming in dogs, and so in many respects, a dog is not as "smart" as a 2-year-old.

Meanwhile, for miffed dog lovers, yes, it is the case that a dog can exhibit "intelligence" that seems to exceed that of a 2-year-old, based on certain kinds of tasks and actions.

All I'm saying is that by using the word "intelligence" you are confounding the comparison and it does little to shed light on a rather meaty subject.

In any case, shift gears one more time and consider what the AI is doing.

Is the AI driving system thinking?

I'd like to debunk a common myth that today's AI systems are somehow able to think and thusly should be compared to human capabilities of thinking.

It's not even close.

Today's AI systems are unarguably a far cry from human thinking and don't fall for malarkey that asserts otherwise.

Conclusion

Overall, by discussing how dogs do driving, it brings up the important point that today's AI systems aren't "thinking" and therefore do not be misled into believing that true self-driving cars have presumably crossed the boundary over into AI that is the same as human thought.

We have not yet reached the so-called singularity, and don't hold your breath waiting for it to happen (though, certainly we can discuss the potential and be debating what to do if that occurs).

It's a dog-eat-dog world that we live in, and even dogs occasionally and fortuitously get their day, including having a chance to drive a car rather than merely chasing one.

This also proves beyond a shadow of a doubt that you can teach an old dog a new trick.

CHAPTER 5
HYPODERMIC NEEDLES AND
AI SELF-DRIVING CARS

CHAPTER 5

HYPODERMIC NEEDLES

AND

AI SELF-DRIVING CARS

Recent news indicates that some workers at a prominent self-driving car company reported that they've found leftover hypodermic needles inside the vehicles (though this report was about Waymo, keep in mind that all of the driverless car makers are subject to the same potential adverse activity).

Apparently, some passengers have opted to use such needles while inside the driverless cars or otherwise decided to "dispose" of the needles by carelessly leaving the dangerous artifacts inside the vehicle.

Maybe the reason for the discarded needles involves illicit drug activity by passengers riding inside a self-driving car or might consist of the more innocuous use of injections by diabetics. Nonetheless, in either case, the thoughtless act of leaving needles laying around inside a car is startling and inexcusable.

Very scary.

Why so?

Besides the potential danger for the driverless car employees that cleanout the interior of the cars, there is a far more widespread concern that this matter poses.

Once self-driving cars are prevalent, we will all likely be riding in them on a ridesharing basis, doing so from time-to-time or a lot of the time, rather than being in a human-driven ridesharing car.

In the case of a human-driven car, one would hope that the driver would either prevent people from using hypodermic needles while inside the car or at least would make sure to clean out the needles prior to picking up their next passenger.

For a true self-driving car, there isn't a human driver in the vehicle.

Thus, if someone opts to leave a hypodermic needle, say dropping it onto the seat or the floor, whoever next comes into the car might find themselves on the worst side of that sordid act.

Bad news.

Furthermore, the next person that uses that ridesharing driverless car might not notice the needle and perchance by luck of the draw does not get pricked by the needle. Thus, it could be that the needle is subtly hidden, and perhaps only after numerous other passengers come and go during the driverless car journey would one be unfortunate enough to discover it.

A silent trap waiting to be sprung.

We all know that getting stuck by a used needle is chancy and could lead to any number of infections, including hepatitis B virus, hepatitis C virus, etc.

For those of you that might be thinking this is a tempest in a teapot since the odds of someone getting pricked is perhaps considered low, and the needle might also have to penetrate several layers of clothing to actually break your skin, I'll add something else that will make your hair stand on end.

Soon, not only will adults be routinely using self-driving cars, but we are also going to have children using self-driving cars too.

Furthermore, oftentimes the children will be in the driverless car without any adult supervision.

I realize that it seems unimaginable that children would ride in a car without adult supervision. Today, there always has to be some adult in the vehicle due to the need to drive the car. With driverless cars, there's no driver and therefore no default adult always inside to watch over minors.

Parents today probably cannot envision allowing their children to ride in a self-driving car san an adult being present. Well, once driverless cars are readily available, it will become a huge temptation to let the kids ride by themselves.

Here's why.

You are at work and your boss refuses to let you leave the office to go pick-up your child from school. All your son or daughter needs is a quick ride over to piano practice. It's just a mere five-minute drive.

So, you hail a ridesharing driverless car to give your child a lift.

What could go wrong?

In theory, assuming that self-driving cars are going to be as safe or even safer than human-driven cars (this is still unknown), it would seem that nothing out of the ordinary could go awry.

There is one potential catch.

A potentially big catch.

Suppose some idiot has left a used hypodermic needle in the car.

Your child gets into the vehicle, unsuspecting that earlier in the day a drug addict had used the car for a nefarious act. Not only could the child accidentally get pricked by the discarded needle, but the child might also unknowingly cause themselves to be stuck by the needle.

How so?

There are numerous reported cases of kids finding needles on playgrounds or in bathrooms that spotted a needle and decided to pick it up.

In some cases, the child was unaware of the danger involved and merely was trying to inspect the needle out of curiosity. In other cases, the child was trying to do the "right thing" by picking up the needle to prevent others from getting stuck and was determined to bring the needle to an adult, yet sadly their effort led to themselves getting pricked.

For those that assert that the self-driving car companies ought to include a special disposal box inside the driverless car, allowing needles to be placed into the container, I'd like to point out that's not much of a solution and can actually backfire.

Let's take the child example and see how that plays out.

An adult with an utter lack of care for other people decides to leave a used needle in the car and either doesn't notice the special disposal box or doesn't give a hoot about it. Meanwhile, a child, later on, gets into the vehicle, spots the needle, and tries to do the "right thing" by picking up the needle to place it into the disposal box.

In that sense, the disposal box ironically could prod a child somewhat to pick-up the needle (I realize you might say that the box should have a sign that says don't touch any needles, but keep in mind that the child either might not read the sign or might opt to ignore the sign).

There's an additional twist too.

Some people that opt to use a self-driving car might see the disposal box and think therefore that it is okay to use a needle while in the driverless car. In essence, the box kind of emits an unstated signal that it is permissible to use needles in the vehicle since otherwise why in the world would the box be there, one might say.

No, the placement of a special disposal box does not solve this problem.

Here's an important question: *How will AI-based true self-driving cars contend with the potential for passengers leaving behind dangerous items that could harm other riders later on?*

Let's unpack the matter and see.

The Levels Of Self-Driving Cars

It is important to clarify what I mean when referring to true self-driving cars.

True self-driving cars are ones that the AI drives the car entirely on its own and there isn't any human assistance during the driving task.

These driverless vehicles are considered a Level 4 and Level 5, while a car that requires a human driver to co-share the driving effort is usually considered at a Level 2 or Level 3. The cars that co-share the driving task are described as being semi-autonomous, and typically contain a variety of automated add-on's that are referred to as ADAS (Advanced Driver-Assistance Systems).

There is not yet a true self-driving car at Level 5, which we don't yet even know if this will be possible to achieve, and nor how long it will take to get there.

Meanwhile, the Level 4 efforts are gradually trying to get some traction by undergoing very narrow and selective public roadway trials, though there is controversy over whether this testing should be allowed per se (we are all life-or-death guinea pigs in an experiment taking place on our highways and byways, some point out).

Since semi-autonomous cars require a human driver, the adoption of those types of cars won't be markedly different than driving conventional vehicles, so there's not much new per se to cover about them on this topic (though, as you'll see in a moment, the points next made are generally applicable).

For semi-autonomous cars, it is important that the public be forewarned about a disturbing aspect that's been arising lately, namely that in spite of those human drivers that keep posting videos of themselves falling asleep at the wheel of a Level 2 or Level 3 car, we all need to avoid being misled into believing that the driver can take away their attention from the driving task while driving a semi-autonomous car.

You are the responsible party for the driving actions of the vehicle, regardless of how much automation might be tossed into a Level 2 or Level 3.

Self-Driving Cars And Leftover Items

For Level 4 and Level 5 true self-driving vehicles, there won't be a human driver involved in the driving task.

All occupants will be passengers.

The AI is doing the driving.

One looming trust-related issue for self-driving cars will be whether people believe that AI-based driving systems are safe enough to drive a car without any human intervention needed.

Let's assume that ultimately there is sufficient evidence and public perception such that people are willing to ride in self-driving cars on a widespread basis.

Great, you say, this means that we are all free-and-clear on having people ride in driverless cars.

Not necessarily so.

As mentioned, if there are instances of needles being leftover in driverless cars, and if someone gets hurt, it could be the so-called bad apple in the barrel that spoils the whole barrel.

In other words, people that otherwise believe a self-driving car is safe will now have second thoughts about the safety, though not due to the driving, but instead ironically enough due to the aspect that without a human driver there is the chance that dangerous items will be left behind in the vehicle.

Some point out that the solution is simple, namely making sure that between each driving journey that there is someone employed by the owner of the driverless fleet that cleans out the vehicle.

Say what?

Think about that solution.

A driverless car is roaming throughout a city, awaiting a request for use.

After picking up a rider and delivering the person to their desired destination, somehow the driverless car needs to now get cleaned by a person employed for that purpose.

This means that the driverless car needs to route itself to wherever this person resides.

This also means that the driverless car is not earning any money while making the trip to the cleaner. Once the driverless car arrives at the cleaner, the employee (or contractor) makes sure that the car is clean and ready to proceed.

During this cleaning time, the self-driving car is not making any money.

In addition to the lost revenue, this also means that the fleet of driverless cars will always have some number of self-driving cars "out of service" throughout the day and night.

In turn, this means that you'll have to wait longer for a self-driving car to arrive and pick you up, or alternatively, the fleet owner will need to deploy an excess number of driverless cars to contend with the non-use time.

There's also the matter of the cost of the labor to clean the cars and renting space where the driverless cars will go to be cleaned. And so on.

The point is that this idea of cleaning after each trip is going to be quite costly (as a side note, the fleet owner will need to have some provision for cleaning their driverless cars, though this presumably will be done on a periodic basis, maybe once per 24 hours or something like that, rather than after each distinct driving journey).

For the case of human-driven cars, presumably, there is already a built-in cleaner per se, the human driver.

Once the human driver is no longer needed, you've excised out the human cleaner being part-and-parcel of the car, so to speak.

Postulating Other Approaches

I've heard some pundits suggest that the passengers ought to be responsible and clean the driverless cars themselves.

Use a reality check on that.

Will we all be expected to clean-up a self-driving car each time that we ride in one?

Plus, once again, if the item left behind is a dangerous item such as a discarded needle, you are now intentionally leading toward having passengers get hurt (that's a lawsuit waiting to happen).

One "compromise" proposed is that the self-driving car will have an OnStar-like service capability, whereby you can press a button to connect with a remote human agent and report that there is a dangerous item in the vehicle, or maybe just tell the AI system via its Natural Language Processing (NLP), akin to talking to Alexa or Siri.

Yes, this certainly helps, but it doesn't fully solve the problem.

For example, an adult gets into the vehicle and doesn't realize there's a needle in there, sits on the needle and gets harmed.

Sure, they could now use the OnStar-like feature to report that they got stuck, and maybe seek medical assistance, and presumably have someone from the fleet come and clean the car, but meanwhile the damage has been done.

The OnStar-like feature is probably more likely to be used once the horse is out of the barn, rather than as a preventative measure.

Another proposed approach would be to have a fleet authorized employee or contractor riding in the self-driving car, a kind of adult chaperone, as it were.

When you get into a self-driving car, this person would greet you and be there in case you need any assistance and serve too to make sure that the self-driving car is always kept clean.

Well, I'm not sure that's going to be warmly received (it might be used on a selective basis, such as when someone needs assistance getting into and out of the vehicle).

Lance B. Eliot

Once again there's the cost issue of the labor involved, and this also then undercuts any sense of privacy that riders might otherwise find attractive about riding in a driverless car (your phone conversations will be overheard, your every move will be watched).

This brings up another possibility.

Self-driving cars are likely to have inward-facing cameras, doing so to allow you to perform Skype-like remote interactions, such as conferring with workers at the office during your morning commute.

The inward-facing cameras also provide a means for the fleet owner to record whatever happens inside a self-driving car, allowing them to catch on tape anyone that marks graffiti on the interior walls or seats.

Some unresolved questions include:
- Will passengers willingly ride in driverless cars that are continually recording them the entire time?
- What will happen to the video recordings and how will the fleet owner make use of the video?
- Will passengers be able to turn off the video, but in that case, won't most do so and undermine the whole intent of having the video capture take place?

It's a slippery slope and one that bodes concerns about privacy intrusion.

In any case, let's assume that people are willing to have the inward-facing cameras watching what they do while inside a driverless car.

In theory, the AI system inspecting the video stream might be able to detect when someone uses a needle and catch them in the act or at least realize that the driverless car will next need to be routed to a cleaning station (thus, in this use case not all driverless cars would be going to the cleaning station, only the cars that the AI suspects might need a cleaning).

If people find it creepy to be watched by the AI system, presumably the fleet owner could hire remote human agents to watch the video feeds, though this would be an enormously massive operation if you really had humans watching all the video of all the driverless cars while transporting passengers (it is assumed that we'll ultimately have millions upon millions of self-driving cars on our roadways).

Conclusion

Automakers and self-driving tech makers are between a rock and a hard place.

Right now, their focus is primarily on making sure that a self-driving car drives safely.

That's vital to the adoption of driverless cars by society.

The "edge case" of dealing with leftover items has yet to get much attention (edge cases are considered not at the core of a problem being solved), partially due to the aspect that the existing tryouts haven't publicly cited the issue and also that today's riders are a selective set that probably is less likely to leave behind dangerous items.

Once self-driving cars are prevalent, this matter is going to become one of the next looming dark clouds over the expanded use of driverless cars.

And it's not just needles that might be leftover.

Suppose someone leaves a loaded gun, which I know sounds ridiculous and extreme, but realize that people at times leave guns laying around their home or have tried to take them onto planes. Though presumably there aren't going to be many instances of someone that leaves a loaded gun behind in a driverless car, if it does happen, and if the result is catastrophic, such an occurrence will open the floodgates on the matter.

Many view this leftover item qualm as quirky and trivial.

I wouldn't be so quick to disregard the matter.

There are various additional ways to try and deal with the problem, and some are trying, though whether any of those are sufficiently sensible, usable, and cost-effective is yet to be ascertained.

Time will tell.

.

CHAPTER 6

SHARING SELF-DRIVING TECH IS NOT LIKELY

CHAPTER 6

SHARING SELF-DRIVING TECH
IS NOT LIKELY

Can't we all work together?

This question is often brought up at conferences on AI self-driving cars.

Why so?

Well, it is noteworthy to realize that there are currently about 40,000 deaths each year in the United States due to car accidents and about 2.5 million injuries that arise via car crashes.

If you believe that the advent of true self-driving cars will reduce the annual number of deaths and injuries, the sooner that we get AI self-driving cars on the road then the sooner we'll start saving precious lives and reducing injuries.

The question posed about working together is essentially a notion that instead of the automakers working on their own to try and achieve self-driving cars, perhaps the task would be completed sooner if all the automakers agreed to openly share with each other.

In a kind of kumbaya moment, akin to at wartime having everyone suddenly lay down their arms, wouldn't it be wonderful if the automakers would divulge everything that they know and are arduously doing toward creating a driverless car, and then the resulting synergy of this massive "open source" approach might speed-up the process?

The point being that today there is a winner beats all mindset, of which each automaker is striving on their own to craft a true self-driving car, but wouldn't we all be winners as a society if the automakers just opened-up the kimono and bared all for everyone else to see their driverless car efforts.

Presumably, they ought to showcase the propriety algorithms that they've devised for self-driving capabilities and post their voluminous AI code in a public forum for all to peruse.

They ought to release the data that they've collected from their roadway trials, providing a treasure trove of data that could allow others to employ Machine Learning and Deep Learning to ferret out ways to best drive a car.

For those using simulations to do testing of their AI driving systems, they ought to allow others to log into the simulation and see what kinds of parameters and settings are being used, along with allowing anyone else to utilize the simulation for the furtherance of their driverless car tech.

Furthermore, one of the biggest hurdles in devising self-driving cars involves figuring out so-called edge cases, involving seemingly unusual or oddball driving circumstances and being able to prepare the AI driving system to cope with those situations.

Rather than each automaker having to figure out edge cases on their own, perhaps it would be best if a large-scale database of known edge cases was formulated and provided access to anyone interested.

Think of how such a collective set would aid others that hadn't yet discovered various edge cases and thus they would not have to reinvent the wheel, so to speak, and could simply refer to the open database instead.

In short, the assumption being that today's rather fragmented and disjointed approach involving singular companies attempting to each develop AI-based self-driving cars could be turned on its head, allowing a grand collective of all such makers that would open their doors and share their proprietary secrets.

Sure, there are some automakers that have already done something like this on a smaller scale, forming partnerships or joining small consortiums of fellow firms, but the notion here is a wholescale and unmitigated sharing and openness by everyone in the industry.

In theory, this would also encompass the people involved too, namely that the AI developers, engineers, scientists, and others would toss aside their company badges and become a member of a national or presumably global collective seeking to produce true self-driving cars.

Many have likened trying to achieve self-driving cars to be like a moonshot, and thus you might suggest that this desire to get everyone to share is akin to asserting that the mission to the moon or similar is so important to humanity that all should reveal their efforts.

Imagine a science fiction movie whereby say the earth is under siege and our only hope is to colonize and live on the moon. As a species, we would want to collectively work together to find a means to lift all humans to the moon and setup moon-based cities for us to live there.

If we don't all pitch in toward the moon mission, it would mean that some humans or perhaps all humans would be wiped out once the threat to earth actually happens.

I'm not suggesting that the lack of achieving self-driving cars is on par with such a cataclysmic saga, and only trying to offer that it is roughly the same kind of logic being employed.

In short, the propositional argument is that the automakers ought to make fully publicly known their self-driving wares since doing so would presumably save lives by sooner achieving driverless cars, based on the assumption that other such firms could all leverage the heretofore secreted and isolated efforts.

We would all use each other's work as steppingstones, climbing up the steep ladder toward driverless cars, together.

I don't want to be the one to burst anyone's bubble, and so allow me to forewarn you that I'm about to say something that could be quite unsettling.

Trigger alert, trigger alert.

That rather starry-eyed altruistic hope is just not going to happen.

It certainly seems like an uplifting humanitarian gesture if it could be done, and maybe it makes sense on a hypothetical basis, but on any practical scale, it's a no-starter.

Today's question then is: *Would it be viable for all automakers and self-driving car tech firms to share everything they've got in order to presumably speed-up the pace of arriving at true self-driving cars?*

For numerous reasons, as I'll argue herein, it isn't a viable proposition.

Let's unpack the matter and see.

The Levels Of Self-Driving Cars

It is important to clarify what I mean when referring to true self-driving cars.

True self-driving cars are ones that the AI drives the car entirely on its own and there isn't any human assistance during the driving task.

These driverless vehicles are considered a Level 4 and Level 5, while a car that requires a human driver to co-share the driving effort is usually considered at a Level 2 or Level 3. The cars that co-share the driving task are described as being semi-autonomous, and typically contain a variety of automated add-on's that are referred to as ADAS (Advanced Driver-Assistance Systems).

There is not yet a true self-driving car at Level 5, which we don't yet even know if this will be possible to achieve, and nor how long it will take to get there.

Meanwhile, the Level 4 efforts are gradually trying to get some traction by undergoing very narrow and selective public roadway trials, though there is controversy over whether this testing should be allowed per se (we are all life-or-death guinea pigs in an experiment taking place on our highways and byways, some point out).

Since semi-autonomous cars require a human driver, the adoption of those types of cars won't be markedly different than driving conventional vehicles, so there's not much new per se to cover about them on this topic (though, as you'll see in a moment, the points next made are generally applicable).

For semi-autonomous cars, it is important that the public be forewarned about a disturbing aspect that's been arising lately, namely that in spite of those human drivers that keep posting videos of themselves falling asleep at the wheel of a Level 2 or Level 3 car, we all need to avoid being misled into believing that the driver can take away their attention from the driving task while driving a semi-autonomous car.

You are the responsible party for the driving actions of the vehicle, regardless of how much automation might be tossed into a Level 2 or Level 3.

Self-Driving Cars And Pace Of Development

For Level 4 and Level 5 true self-driving vehicles, there won't be a human driver involved in the driving task.

All occupants will be passengers.

The AI is doing the driving.

As might be apparent by reading the headlines of the news, promises of being able to achieve Level 4 and Level 5 have been made and then broken, repeatedly, and some are beginning to wonder whether the any-day-now predictions hold any water.

As such, those that proffer the question about whether to open the kimono are sincerely grasping for a means to get things further prodded along.

Consider though the reverse side of the question.

Why would automakers want to openly share all of their hard-fought-for and expensively devised propriety tech about driverless cars?

Think of it this way.

Shareholders of automakers and self-driving car tech firms have bought those stocks under the belief that it is a sensible investment. If you invested in automaker X, and automaker X is able to achieve driverless cars, the stock that you hold would presumably rise in valuation as a kind of reward for the automaker having arrived at such a goal.

And, the automakers themselves have likely already invested millions upon millions of dollars, in some cases billions, toward their self-driving car development efforts.

If they laid bare all their proprietary efforts, it essentially would mean that they have tossed away their investments, and it means that other firms that didn't make such investments are now the richer for it.

Yes, maybe this would be for the collective good, but it would pretty much undermine and even wipe out the firms that long fought to try and make driverless cars.

The shareholders would likely lose their shirts, the automakers would see a precipitous drop in their valuations, and you'd be rewarding others that hadn't devoted time and money in the same manner.

In fact, a strong case could be made of malfeasance toward the management teams and operating officers, and boards of directors, due to simply giving away their valuable assets.

So, the first argument in opposition to the open kimono notion is that there's really little or no financial incentive for the automakers to do so, and likely a humongous financial penalty if they did so.

Next, let's consider whether the collective approach is really going to get you what you want.

In other words, the base assumption is that by collectively sharing everything known about AI self-driving cars, we would be better off and sooner able to achieve driverless cars.

That's not necessarily the case.

Right now, there are Darwinian juices spurring each of the automakers toward the goal of achieving true self-driving cars.

There are billions of dollars to be made, perhaps trillions of dollars, and the pot of gold is enabling automakers to spend their precious time and money accordingly.

If all automakers were going to at all times bare all on their driverless car efforts, what is the incentive for them to continue to strive mightily in that direction?

Suggesting that they ought to want to save lives is a nice idea, and certainly they would all agree that is indeed vital, but if it suggests that none of them will make money to remain in business or they will make smaller money due to a splintering of the driverless pie, you are knocking out a key motivation that keeps the engines running on achieving self-driving cars.

And, here's a crucial point, having everything on the table about self-driving cars is not necessarily going to speed-up development.

It could have the opposite effect.

There might be so much to choose from, and the myriad of approaches so diverse, you could end up with a breadth approach rather than a focused approach, and slow down development accordingly.

Too much of a good thing, one might say.

Think too of the complexities involved in somehow coordinating across all of the industry.

Who decides that these set of sensors are the "best" approach for achieving self-driving cars, or that algorithms N and M are the best choices?

You could say that just let whoever do whatever they want, but this would seem to be a muddled way to proceed, and it would be less likely to go as fast as would the existing focused efforts.

Some might counter-argue that a special conglomerate could be established and become the centralized overseer of the aims to achieve self-driving cars.

Maybe each automaker would get a share of the conglomerate as based on the value of the driverless tech that they contribute to the collective.

Well, I'll just say that this would become a huge drain of time and attention, while everyone fights for their relative apportionment, and the odds are it would distract from the efforts underway to arrive at true self-driving cars.

One would also have to wonder whether this special conglomerate might get bogged down and by its own weight become a barrier to advancing on self-driving cars.

More Considerations

Let's consider some additional reasons why the grand sharing approach is not especially viable.

If sharing is so compelling and it has to do with saving lives, one must ask why the same question doesn't get pressed in other domains.

For example, there are about 635,000 deaths each year in the United States due to heart disease. That's readily over ten times the car-related deaths of 40,000 each year in the U.S.

Why not go after the medical and healthcare field and assert that if they all openly shared their proprietary efforts it would save lives?

If you ponder that question, you'll see that once again the rebuttal arguments mentioned herein about doing so for self-driving cars are equally applicable.

Shifting gears, another aspect to consider is that the efforts toward conventional cars becoming safer will presumably continue to reduce the annual number of deaths and injuries of car accidents.

Step by step, by adding additional safety-related features to conventional cars, the impact of car crashes can be lessened.

This has the potential of closing the gap toward the advantages that true self-driving cars might provide.

In essence, suppose that conventional cars become "safer" and that the number of deaths and injuries is reduced by some percentage Y. If the basis for wanting to open-up self-driving car tech is that it is intended to save lives, the conventional approach might have already lessened to some degree the volume involved (note that all lives are precious and so it is awkward and difficult to argue about net lives savings, though it is a harsh reality when considering these kinds of matters).

Conclusion

Don't misinterpret this analysis to somehow suggest that automakers ought to work only in isolation of each other.

That's not the point.

In fact, as earlier mentioned, there is a continual effort going on of various automakers forming into teams with other automakers, though as can be seen by the tensions often involved that it is a lot harder to do than it might seem on paper.

Plus, there is a lot of hiring of AI self-driving car developers that go across the street from one automaker to the other, thus in a more subtle way perhaps bringing about sharing (albeit one that often generates lawsuits involving claims of having "stolen" propriety matters).

There are lots of conferences and events about self-driving cars that bring together disparate automakers, allowing for a narrow kind of sharing. In addition, there is the academic world and its efforts on self-driving car advances that frequently are relatively openly being shared.

And, for those of you that have kept up with the movement toward open-source, there have been some efforts in the self-driving car realm toward leveraging open-source approaches (examples include openpilot, apollo, carla, etc.). This though is generally of a limited nature and scope, and not on par with the starry-eyed overarching notion being floated.

All told the wishful thinking that all automakers and self-driving car tech firms ought to make available whatever they have is a bit fantastical and utterly unrealistic.

For those that harbor this impossible dream, I wish you well but gently urge that your energies might be better spent in other ways.

Of course, if we could create AI that's super-intelligent, maybe we would ask it to devise AI self-driving cars for us.

Thus, rather us humans right now myopically focusing on achieving AI-based self-driving cars, let's instead aim at developing super-intelligent AI that can get the job done for us.

Solved that problem.

CHAPTER 7

UBER DRIVER "KIDNAPPING" IS SELF-DRIVING LESSON

CHAPTER 7

UBER DRIVER "KIDNAPPING" IS SELF-DRIVING LESSON

Did you happen to watch or hear about one of this week's most harrowing escapades involving an Uber driver that went out of his mind?

Befitting perhaps that it was the week of Valentine's Day, the saga includes a date-night couple that had arranged for babysitters to watch their kids so they could have a fun night on the town.

Well, it was quite a night, that's for sure.

Here's the scoop.

After getting into an Uber ride, the couple settled into the backseat and expected nothing more than a quiet journey for their romantic date-night frolic.

Unfortunately, the Uber car after driving a few blocks got into a minor fender bender while in traffic (rear-ended), doing so without any particular bodily injuries and nor any substantive damage to the vehicles involved.

You might think that the story ends there, but it's just the beginning.

Turns out that the other driver decided to speed-off, avoiding the usual effort of stopping to make sure everyone is okay and exchanging automobile insurance info.

What did the Uber driver do?

He could have pulled over, made sure his passengers were okay, and perhaps then called 911 to report the incident and see if the police could find the car that sped away.

That would seem to be the right thing to do.

Instead, the Uber driver decided it was time to do an all-out car chase through the streets of downtown Richmond, Virginia.

Yes, he jammed his accelerator pedal to the floor and opted to do a veritable fast-and-furious, driving wildly, and pursuing the other car through red lights and endangering everyone along the way.

It became a nightmare for pedestrians that happened to be near the roadways, risking getting hit as the cars weaved and raced through intersections and unprotected crosswalks.

Other cars and their drivers and passengers were also endangered.

All because the Uber driver was determined to catch-up with the other car.

It makes you wonder about the motivation.

Was it based on watching way too many cop movies and spy films?

Does he regularly play the video game Grand Theft Auto and it went to his head?

Had he been in other car crashes and the road rage seething in him finally came to a boil?

Perhaps it was his form of street justice, and he might have reasoned that if the driver hit his car, they were undoubtedly a menace to the highways and byways and so it made sense to go and capture the dastardly criminal.

Of course, he might not have used his noggin at all and merely reacted in the spur of the moment.

Either way, it was an Uber ride of a lifetime for the date-night couple (and hopefully the only time they'll ever have such an experience).

You see, the Uber driver wouldn't let them out of his car.

They pleaded with him, repeatedly, and yelled to let them out.

No dice, the Uber driver seemed to be thinking, since if he came to a stop and let them out, he'd likely lose the pursuit and the scoundrel would have gotten away.

Believe it or not, the Uber driver seemed to somewhat "acquiesce" by calling 911 on his cell phone, incredibly so during the high-speed antics and handed his smartphone to the date-night couple. While on the speaker of the phone, the couple told the 911 operator what was happening, and the 911 agent insistently told the Uber driver that the car should be brought to a halt.

This seemed to fall on deaf ears, and the Uber driver continued unabated.

At one point, while in the midst of the crazy chase, the Uber car got T-boned by a car that was an innocent in these matters and simply and regrettably was in the wrong place at the wrong time.

Eventually, the Uber driver stopped the car and let the couple out.

It almost seems like a dream or one of those concocted Hollywood scripts, but the thing is that the date-night couple decided to live stream the encounter on Facebook, providing sufficient proof of the scary foray.

In case you think that this might be one of those faked or staged videos to try and generate views, the video sure seems to be true, plus the couple reported the matter to the police and if they falsified the whole thing they'd be at risk of strict prosecution.

On the video you can hear the wife of the couple telling the Uber driver that she was worried for their lives and she also pleaded that they have children and that the possibility of never seeing them again wasn't something they had planned on occurring that night.

It seems that overall no one was seriously injured in the convoluted and distressing ordeal, thankfully.

So far, it appears that the driver of the initial car crash and the original impetus for the chase is still at large.

After the incident was over, Uber later indicated that they've now discontinued the Uber driver's access to the Uber network, and Uber officials say they ready to aid the police in the formal investigation of the incident.

What makes the story so unnerving is the fact that the Uber driver would not let the couple out of his car during the erratic and perilous car chase.

If he alone had undertaken the car chase, I doubt that we'd have heard about the incident. It would be just another story of some nutty driver pursuing some other nutty driver.

In essence, the Uber driver "kidnapped" the date-night couple.

Indeed, many are calling for kidnapping charges to be lodged against the Uber driver.

Take a moment to contemplate the nature of this presumed kidnapping action.

Could it happen to you?

Sure, the same kind of thing could readily happen to you.

Whenever you get into a car and have someone else driving the car, there's always the possibility that they might decide to hit the gas and take you along for a ride, whether you want it to happen or not.

Getting into a car that's driven by a family member or a friend or colleague is usually a relatively safe act since you know the person and would hopefully be aware of whether they might snap and kidnap you on a wild ride.

The rub is that when you get into a ride-sharing car or a taxi or any vehicle driven by a stranger, you really have no idea what they might do.

You are betting that they won't do anything rash, otherwise they might lose their license to drive or undermine their driving livelihood.

Despite that theoretical barrier that would usually prevent someone from driving in a kidnapping manner, there's always a chance that it can nonetheless occur.

Bottom-line is that you as a passenger are completely vulnerable to the human driver at the wheel.

For those of you believing that you could take over the wheel, good luck on that thinking. It might work well in the movies, but in a moving car and with the other driver resisting, the odds are that any entanglement with the driver is going to have as bad an outcome as you might otherwise anticipate in the whole situation.

Nope, overpowering a crazed driver is not much of an option.

The odds are that you either talk the driver out of their frantic activity, or you try to bail out of the car when feasible, though at high speeds you are nearly at the same amount of risk as staying inside the car and hoping for the best.

Mull over how much risk we take on each day in this regard, let it sink in, heavily.

If we are all constantly at risk due to being at the whim of human drivers that drive us around, it brings up a rather interesting question to be pondered.

Since true self-driving cars are going to be driven by an AI system, this eliminates the use of a human driver in the car.

Here's the question for the day: *Will the advent of AI-based true self-driving cars mean that you can never again be "kidnapped" by a driver?*

Let's unpack the matter and see.

The Levels Of Self-Driving Cars

It is important to clarify what I mean when referring to true self-driving cars.

True self-driving cars are ones that the AI drives the car entirely on its own and there isn't any human assistance during the driving task.

These driverless vehicles are considered a Level 4 and Level 5, while a car that requires a human driver to co-share the driving effort is usually considered at a Level 2 or Level 3. The cars that co-share the driving task are described as being semi-autonomous, and typically contain a variety of automated add-on's that are referred to as ADAS (Advanced Driver-Assistance Systems).

There is not yet a true self-driving car at Level 5, which we don't yet even know if this will be possible to achieve, and nor how long it will take to get there.

Meanwhile, the Level 4 efforts are gradually trying to get some traction by undergoing very narrow and selective public roadway trials, though there is controversy over whether this testing should be allowed per se (we are all life-or-death guinea pigs in an experiment taking place on our highways and byways, some point out).

Since semi-autonomous cars require a human driver, the adoption of those types of cars won't be markedly different than driving conventional vehicles, so there's not much new per se to cover about them on this topic (though, as you'll see in a moment, the points next made are generally applicable).

For semi-autonomous cars, it is important that the public be forewarned about a disturbing aspect that's been arising lately, namely that in spite of those human drivers that keep posting videos of themselves falling asleep at the wheel of a Level 2 or Level 3 car, we all need to avoid being misled into believing that the driver can take away their attention from the driving task while driving a semi-autonomous car.

You are the responsible party for the driving actions of the vehicle, regardless of how much automation might be tossed into a Level 2 or Level 3.

Self-Driving Cars And The Gun-Toting Kidnapper

For Level 4 and Level 5 true self-driving vehicles, there won't be a human driver involved in the driving task.

All occupants will be passengers.

The AI is doing the driving.

Thank goodness, you might exclaim since this means that no longer can a nutty human driver entrap you in a car and kidnap you during a wild ride.

Well, maybe, maybe not.

It is true that there's not a human driver involved.

But, if someone with a gun got into a driverless car with you, and pointed the gun at you, presumably you could be kidnapped while inside a self-driving car.

Your first thought is that this seems mightily contrived.

I wouldn't be so quick to dismiss the idea out-of-hand.

In today's world, we don't see much of this kind of gunpoint in-car kidnapping.

You might remember that a few years ago that carjackings became a momentary trend and people became quite concerned about a gun touting thug that might try to take your car. The hooligan would either tell you to get out of your car and steal it from you, or they might tell you to keep driving and take them where they want to go. The other possibility was that they might hold the gun on you while they are driving, a more difficult feat, and keep you imprisoned during a driving journey.

Those last two options mean that you are a kidnapping victim (if they take your car, you technically weren't kidnapped and instead your car was stolen from you).

Fortunately, it seems like carjackings are now a rarity.

You'll be both displeased and taken aback to know that there's a term now added to our vocabulary for the instance of the same thing happening via a driverless car, it's known as a _robojacking_ (a semi-clever conjoining of the advent of robot or driverless cars and the idea of kidnapping, see **more at this link**).

Robojacking To Arise

Here's how a robojacking might happen.

You request a driverless car to take you to the local grocery store.

When the self-driving car arrives to pick you up, there's a person already in the vehicle, whom you presume is going to get out of the driverless car. Instead, after you've opened the car door, they stick a gun in your face and tell you to get into the vehicle.

That's version number one.

Version number two is that you request a driverless car, get into it, and start upon your driving journey.

When the self-driving car pulls up to a stop sign, it dutifully comes to a full stop.

A thug then opens the door of the driverless car and while pointing a gun tells you to move over so they can ride along with you.

I realize you are thinking that you'd always keep the doors locked while riding in a driverless car. Yes, that might help, but if the gun-toting evil-doer points the gun at you, while the driverless car is stopped at the stop sign, and the menacing hoodlum yells at you to open the door, you've got to ask yourself one question, namely, do you open the door or not?

If you don't open the door, maybe the outlaw shoots you dead through the window.

Not desirable.

Anyway, it will be a dilemma, that's for sure.

Okay, you say, if that's going to possibly happen, why doesn't it happen nowadays?

Here's the twist.

If a human is driving a car and a gun-wielding nut aims their revolver at the car, the odds are that the human driver is going to radially maneuver the car to avoid the offender.

There's still a chance of the shooter opting to shoot at you, but now at least you have some chance to get away or reduce the odds of getting shot point-blank. By and large, you can turn the car into a weapon to confront the weapon being pointed at you. The car becomes either a threat to the gun-carrying villain or at least a means of potential escape.

Right now, an AI self-driving car is none of those things.

Most of the AI driverless cars would simply carry on as though nothing is amiss.

They won't deduce that there's a person with a gun that's threatening the passengers of the driverless car (see more about this kind of AI limitation and the lack of being able to cope with active shooter situations).

I know that some of you are thinking that the AI will certainly embody an escape artist driver and pull out all the stops to save you, but that's not in the cards for now (the automakers and self-driving car tech firms are struggling just to get a car to drive legally and properly, let alone deal with an "edge" case of saving your life from a nut with a gun).

Self-driving cars will have an Alexa or Siri kind of Natural Language Processing (NLP) capability, allowing you to verbally indicate where you want to be driven, and as such, you might assume that you could urgently tell the AI system to zoom away and escape the shadowy figure standing outside the car.

Well, here's the bad news, many of the top executives at the firms developing self-driving cars are saying that the only commands you can utter to the AI involve where it is to go. All of the driving aspects are going to be done by the AI system and without any human intervention.

Why?

First, because its harder to make the NLP deal with human vagaries of what humans might ask the AI to do (this though, in my view, does not serve as a valid excuse, as I've exhorted over and over again).

Second, they don't want the passengers telling the AI to hit the gas or jam on the brakes since the passengers might be wrong or they might be desirous of running over an innocent person, or maybe the rider is intoxicated and has no idea what they are saying.

In that case, the baby is being thrown out with the bathwater since this also means that you cannot persuade the AI to dodge a gun-wielding maniac that is threatening you.

I'll make you even sicker about the matter.

Realize that the AI is trying to be purely street legal, at least as it has been presumably programmed to do (I've pointed out this is also a false and misleading notion).

Why does this matter?

If a human driver saw a person with a gun standing at a stop sign, the odds are that a human driver might exercise discretion and drive right through the stop and not have the car come to a halt, when doing so was more dangerous than simply running the stop sign itself.

Guess what?

The AI is going to come to a stop at the stop sign, no matter what, at least as it is being programmed today.

Furthermore, worse still, even if the driverless car isn't coming up to a stop sign, all the robojacker needs to do is step into the street like a jaywalker.

A human driver would likely aim to run over the jaywalking gun-toting nut, or at least seem to do so, perhaps getting the nut to leap away in a game of chicken, but an AI self-driving car is going to dutifully come to a halt so as to avoid hitting a human jaywalker.

What today is becoming a "prank" by those that live near where driverless cars are being fielded, such as getting a driverless car to come to a sudden halt or weave away from you, will become a means to pretty much outright robojack a driverless car.

Not desirable.

Conclusion

There are various other aspects involved in this somewhat complicated matter.

For example, driverless cars are likely to have an OnStar-like capability that you can invoke as a passenger, and perhaps a remote human operator can take over the controls of the car (which, is not necessarily going to be a good thing).

It is doubtful that if a gun aiming murderer is trying to stop you while inside a driverless car that you'll be able to invoke the OnStar-like feature and chat calmly with the remote agent, doing so expeditiously enough to have the third-party remote driver take needed corrective action on a timely basis.

I wouldn't want to bet my life on it, that's for sure.

In the end, the odds are that we need to have better AI.

The AI driving the car can potentially undertake the same kinds of evasive and threatening actions that a human driver could do, but the problem is a rather thorny one because we also don't want the AI to be able to willy nilly take such actions (in which case, we are "arming" the AI to possibly do very harmful acts, when we presumably don't want it to do so).

Realize too that there isn't any kind of common-sense reasoning as yet robustly devised for today's AI systems.

We are going to see the gradual elimination of human driving, though it also means that many of the "benefits" of having human judgment in driving will either go away or be less fluent until AI systems become more capable.

If the aforementioned worries you about AI-based driving systems, I'll close this topic for now with something else for you to chew on.

Assuming we do achieve a more robust AI capability, suppose the AI itself decides to kidnap you, or some dastardly hacker convinces the AI driving system to do so.

That should really make your hair stand on end.

But that's a story for another day.

CHAPTER 8
GENDER DRIVING BIASES IN AI SELF-DRIVING CARS

CHAPTER 8

GENDER DRIVING BIASES IN AI SELF-DRIVING CARS

Do you think that men are better drivers than women, or do you believe that women are better drivers than men?

Seems like most of us have an opinion on the matter, one way or another.

In a stereotypical manner, men are often characterized as fierce drivers that have a take-no-prisoners attitude, while women supposedly are more forgiving and civil in their driving actions. Depending on how extreme you want to take these tropes, there are some that would say that women shouldn't be allowed on our roadways due to their timidity, while the same could be said that men should not be at the wheel due to their crazed pedal-to-the-metal predilection.

What do the stats say?

According to the latest U.S. Department of Transportation data, based on their FARS or Fatality Analysis Reporting System, the number of males annually killed in car crashes is nearly twice that of the number of females killed in car crashes.

Ponder that statistic for a moment.

Some would argue that it definitely is evidence that male drivers are worse drivers than female drivers, which seems logically sensible under the assumption that since more males are being killed in car crashes than women, men must be getting into a lot more car crashes, ergo they must be worse drivers.

Presumably, it would seem that women are better able to avoid getting into death-producing car crashes, thus they are more adept at driving and are altogether safer drivers.

Whoa, exclaim some that don't interpret the data in that way.

Maybe women are somehow able to survive deadly car crashes better than men, and therefore it isn't fair to compare the count of how many perished.

Or, here's one to get your blood boiling, perhaps women trigger car crashes by disrupting traffic flow and are not being agile enough at the driving controls, and somehow men pay a dear price by getting into deadly accidents while contending with that kind of driving obfuscation.

There seems to be little evidentiary support for those contentions.

A more straightforward counterargument is that men tend to drive more miles than women.

By the very fact that men are on the roadways more so than women, they are obviously going to be vulnerable to a heightened risk of getting into bad car crashes. In a sense, it's a situation of rolling the dice more times than women do.

Insurance companies opt for that interpretation, including too that the stats show that men are more likely to drive while intoxicated, they are more likely to be speeding, they are more likely to not use seatbelts, etc.

There could be additional hidden factors involved in these outcomes.

For example, some studies suggest that the gender differences begin to dissipate with aging, namely that at older ages, the chances of getting killed in a car crash becomes about equal for both male and female drivers.

Of course, even that measure has controversy, which for some it is a sign that men lose their driving edge and spirit as they get older, become more akin to the skittishness of women.

Yikes, it's all a can of worms and a topic that can readily lend itself to fisticuffs.

Suppose there were some means to do away with all human driving and we had only AI-based driving that took place.

One would assume that the AI would not fall into any gender-based camp.

In other words, since we all think of AI as a kind of machine, it wouldn't seem to make much sense to say that an AI system is male or that an AI system is female.

As an aside, there have been numerous expressed concerns that the AI-fostered Natural Language Processing (NLP) systems that are increasingly permeating our lives are perhaps falling into a gender trap, as it were.

When you hear an Alexa or Siri voice that speaks to you if it has a male intonation do you perceive the system in a manner differently than if it has a female intonation?

Some believe that if every time you want to learn something new that you invoke an NLP that happens to have said a female sounding voice, it will tend to cause children especially to start to believe that women are the sole arbiters of the world's facts. This could also work in other ways such as if the female sounding NLP was telling you to do your homework, would that cause kids to be leery of women as though they are always being bossy?

The same can be said about using a male voice for today's NLP systems. If a male-sounding voice is always used, perhaps the context of what the NLP system is telling you might be twisted into being associated with males versus females.

As a result, some argue that the NLP systems ought to have gender-neutral sounding voices.

The aim is to get away from the potential of having people try to stereotype human males and human females by stripping out the gender element from our verbally interactive AI systems.

There's another perhaps equally compelling reason for wanting to excise any male or female intonation from an NLP system, namely that we might tend to anthropomorphize the AI system, unduly so.

Here's what that means.

AI systems are not yet even close to being intelligent, and yet the more that AI systems have the appearance of human-like qualities, we are bound to assume that the AI is as intelligent as humans.

Thus, when you interact with Alexa or Siri, and it uses either a male or female intonation, the argument is that the male or female verbalization acts as a subtle and misleading signal that the underlying system is human-like and ergo intelligent.

You fall readily for the notion that Alexa or Siri must be smart, simply by extension of the aspect that it has a male or female sounding embodiment.

In short, there is ongoing controversy about whether or not the expanding use of NLP systems in our society ought to not "cheat" by using a male or female sounding basis and instead should be completely neutralized in terms of the spoken word and not lean toward using either gender.

Getting back to the topic of AI driving systems, there's a chance that the advent of true self-driving cars might encompass gender traits, akin to how there's concern about Alexa and Siri doing so.

Say what?

You might naturally be puzzled as to why AI driving systems would include any kind of gender specificity.

Here's the question for today's analysis: *Will AI-based true self-driving cars be male, female, gender fluid, or gender-neutral when it comes to the act of driving?*

Let's unpack the matter and see.

The Levels Of Self-Driving Cars

It is important to clarify what I mean when referring to true self-driving cars.

True self-driving cars are ones that the AI drives the car entirely on its own and there isn't any human assistance during the driving task.

These driverless vehicles are considered a Level 4 and Level 5, while a car that requires a human driver to co-share the driving effort is usually considered at a Level 2 or Level 3. The cars that co-share the driving task are described as being semi-autonomous, and typically contain a variety of automated add-on's that are referred to as ADAS (Advanced Driver-Assistance Systems).

There is not yet a true self-driving car at Level 5, which we don't yet even know if this will be possible to achieve, and nor how long it will take to get there.

Meanwhile, the Level 4 efforts are gradually trying to get some traction by undergoing very narrow and selective public roadway trials, though there is controversy over whether this testing should be allowed per se (we are all life-or-death guinea pigs in an experiment taking place on our highways and byways, some point out).

Since semi-autonomous cars require a human driver, the adoption of those types of cars won't be markedly different than driving conventional vehicles, so there's not much new per se to cover about them on this topic (though, as you'll see in a moment, the points next made are generally applicable).

For semi-autonomous cars, it is important that the public be forewarned about a disturbing aspect that's been arising lately, namely that in spite of those human drivers that keep posting videos of themselves falling asleep at the wheel of a Level 2 or Level 3 car, we all need to avoid being misled into believing that the driver can take away their attention from the driving task while driving a semi-autonomous car.

You are the responsible party for the driving actions of the vehicle, regardless of how much automation might be tossed into a Level 2 or Level 3.

Self-Driving Cars And Gender Biases

For Level 4 and Level 5 true self-driving vehicles, there won't be a human driver involved in the driving task.

All occupants will be passengers.

The AI is doing the driving.

At first glance, it seems on the surface that the AI is going to drive like a machine does, doing so without any type of gender influence or bias.

How could gender get somehow shoehorned into the topic of AI driving systems?

There are several ways that the nuances of gender could seep into the matter.

We'll start with the acclaimed use of Machine Learning (ML) or Deep Learning (DL).

As you've likely heard or read, part of the basis for today's rapidly expanding use of AI is partially due to the advances made in ML/DL.

You might have also heard or read that one of the key underpinnings of ML/DL is the need for data, lots and lots of data.

In essence, ML/DL is a computational pattern matching approach.

You feed lots of data into the algorithms being used, and patterns are sought to be discovered. Based on those patterns, the ML/DL can then henceforth potentially detect in new data those same patterns and report as such that those patterns were found.

If I feed tons and tons of pictures that have a rabbit somewhere in each photo into an ML/DL system, the ML/DL can potentially statistically ascertain that a certain shape and color and size of a blob in those photos is a thing that we would refer to as a rabbit.

Please note that the ML/DL is not likely using any human-like common-sense reasoning, which is something not often pointed out about these AI-based systems.

For example, the ML/DL won't "know" that a rabbit is a cute furry animal and that we like to play with them and around Easter, they are especially revered.

Instead, the ML/DL simply based on mathematical computations has calculated that a blob in a picture can be delineated, and possibly readily detected whenever you feed a new picture into the system, attempting to probabilistically state whether there's such a blob present or not.

There's no higher-level reasoning per se, and we are a long ways away from the day when human-like reasoning of that nature is going to be embodied into AI systems (which, some argue, maybe we won't ever achieve, while others keep saying that the day of the grand singularity is nearly upon us).

In any case, suppose that we fed pictures of only white-furry rabbits into the ML/DL when we were training it to find the rabbit blobs in the images.

One aspect that might arise would be that the ML/DL would associate the rabbit blob as always and only being white in color.

When we later on fed in new pictures, the ML/DL might fail to detect a rabbit if it was one that had black fur, because the lack of white fur diminished the calculated chances that the blob was a rabbit (as based on the training set that was used).

In a prior piece, I emphasized that one of the dangers about using ML/DL is the possibility of getting stuck on various biases, such as the aspect that true self-driving cars could end up with a form of racial bias, due to the data that the AI driving system was trained on.

Lo and behold, it is also possible that an AI driving system could incur a gender-related bias.

Here's how.

If you believe that men drive differently than women, and likewise that women drive differently than men, suppose that we collected a bunch of driving-related data that was based on human driving and thus within the data there was a hidden element, specifically that some of the driving was done by men and some of the driving was done by women.

Letting loose an ML/DL system on this dataset, the ML/DL is aiming to try and find driving tactics and strategies as embodied in the data.

Excuse me for a moment as I leverage the stereotypical gender-differences to make my point.

It could be that the ML/DL discovers "aggressive" driving tactics that are within the male-oriented driving data and will incorporate such a driving approach into what the true self-driving car will do while on the roadways.

This could mean that when the driverless car roams on our streets, it is going to employ a male-focused driving style and presumably try to cut off other drivers in traffic, and otherwise be quite pushy.

Or, it could be that the ML/DL discovers the "timid" driving tactics that are within the female-oriented driving data and will incorporate a driving approach accordingly, such that when a self-driving car gets in traffic, the AI is going to act in a more docile manner.

I realize that the aforementioned seems objectionable due to the stereotypical characterizations, but the overall point is that if there is a difference between how males tend to drive and how females tend to drive, it could potentially be reflected in the data.

And, if the data has such differences within it, there's a chance that the ML/DL might either explicitly or implicitly pick-up on those differences.

Imagine too that if we had a dataset that perchance was based only on male drivers, this landing on a male-oriented bias driving approach would seem even more heightened (similarly, if the dataset was based only on female drivers, a female-oriented bias would be presumably heightened).

Here's the rub.

Since male drivers today have twice the number of deadly car crashes than women, if an AI true self-driving car was perchance trained to drive via predominantly male-oriented driving tactics, would the resulting driverless car be more prone to car accidents than otherwise?

That's an intriguing point and worth pondering.

Assuming that no other factors come to play in the nature of the AI driving system, we might certainly reasonably assume that the driverless car so trained might indeed falter in a similar way to the underlying "learned" driving behaviors.

Admittedly, there are a lot of other factors involved in the crafting of an AI driving system, and thus it is hard to say that training datasets themselves could lead to such a consequence.

That being said, it is also instructive to realize that there are other ways that gender-based elements could get infused into the AI driving system.

For example, suppose that rather than only using ML/DL, there was also programming, or coding involved in the AI driving system, which indeed is most often the case.

It could be that the AI developers themselves would allow their own biases to be encompassed into the coding, and since by-and-large stats indicate that AI software developers tend to be males rather than females (though, thankfully, lots of STEM efforts are helping to change this dynamic), perhaps their male-oriented perspective would get included into the AI system coding.

In The Field Biases Too

Yet another example involves the AI dealing with other drivers on the roadways.

For many years to come, we will have both self-driving cars on our highways and byways and simultaneously have human-driven cars. There won't be a magical overnight switch of suddenly having no human-driven cars and only AI driverless cars.

Presumably, self-driving cars are supposed to be crafted to learn from the driving experiences encountered while on the roadways.

Generally, this involves the self-driving car collecting its sensory data during driving journeys, and then uploading the data via OTA (Over-The-Air) electronic communications into the cloud of the automaker or self-driving tech firm. Then, the automaker or self-driving tech firm uses various tools to analyze the voluminous data, including likely ML/DL and pushes out to the fleet of driverless cars some updates based on what was gleaned from the roadway data collected.

How does this pertain to gender?

Assuming again that male drivers and female drivers do drive differently, the roadway experiences of the driverless cars will involve the driving aspects of the human-driven cars around them.

It is quite possible that the ML/DL doing analyses of the fleet collected data would discover the male-oriented or the female-oriented driving tactics, though it and the AI developers might not realize that the deeply buried patterns were somehow tied to gender.

Indeed, one of the qualms about today's ML/DL is that it oftentimes is not amenable to explanation.

The complexity of the underlying computations does not necessarily lend itself to readily being interpreted or explained in everyday ways (for how the need for XAI or Explainable AI is becoming increasingly important).

Conclusion

Some people affectionately refer to their car as a "he" or a "she," as though the car itself was of a particular gender.

When an AI system is at the wheel of a self-driving car, it could be that the "he" or "she" labeling might be applicable, at least in the aspect that the AI driving system could be gender-biased toward male-oriented driving or female-oriented driving (if you believe such a difference exists).

Some believe that the AI driving system will be gender fluid, meaning that based on all the means by which the AI system "learns" to drive, it will blend together the driving tactics that might be ascribed as male-oriented and those that might be ascribed as female-oriented.

If you don't buy into the notion that there is any male versus female driving differences, presumably the AI will be gender-neutral in its driving practices.

No matter what your gender driving beliefs might be, one thing is clear that the whole topic can drive one crazy.

CHAPTER 9

SLAIN BEFRIENDED DOLPHINS ARE SELF-DRIVING LESSONS

CHAPTER 9

SLAIN BEFRIENDED DOLPHINS
ARE SELF-DRIVING LESSONS

Recent news reports indicate that several dolphins in the waters of Florida have been killed by some kind of sharp objects or possibly even bullets that were shot at them (forensic pathologists are still studying the deceased marine mammals).

There is now a $20,000 reward being offered by the National Oceanic and Atmospheric Administration (NOAA) for anyone that can lead authorities to the dastardly scoundrels that undertook the killings.

Let's all hope that the dolphin killings will come to a stop and that the culprits will be found and brought to justice.

There is an added twist to the story that provides additional controversy.

It appears that the dolphins were harmed while in a posture known as the dolphin begging position.

Essentially, when a dolphin is seeking to get fed by a human, the normal action of the dolphin consists of turning onto its side and having its head slightly above the water, which has been dubbed its begging position.

Consider this facet for a moment.

Imagine a dog that has been fed by humans and how it would over time adopt a posture or positioning that it knew was most satisfying to the humans feeding it. Perhaps the dog would go into a sitting stance, panting and expectantly eyeballing a human that is holding outward in their hand scrumptious dogfood.

Of course, the dog might go into the same position even if a human did not have food at-hand, doing so in hopes of sparking the human to provide something to eat.

Or, the human might trick the dog into getting into its eating posture, simply by appearing to have dog food and making motions to suggest as such.

In terms of the dolphins, since the points of attack on their bodies suggest that the mammals were in the begging position, it seems plausible that the dolphins were reacting to the presence of humans that the animals assumed were likely to feed them.

All in all, logically, the dolphins might have readily approached their attackers and did so under the assumption of being fed, including that they remained quite vulnerable to attack via getting quite close to the attackers and showcasing their underbellies.

Experts on bottlenose dolphins say that the begging position is a learned behavior based on wild dolphins having encountered humans that seek to feed the animals.

Furthermore, such experts repeatedly exhort that humans should not be feeding wild dolphins.

First, it undermines the natural efforts of the dolphins, causing the dolphins to seek out humans for survival and to get food, rather than foraging in their own habitat. They become less capable of getting food on their own, plus they often expend precious energy trying to reach humans since doing so provides a presumed "easy" food source.

Second, the dolphins approach humans with an expectation of getting fed, which can cause a kind of vicious cycle whereby humans feed the dolphins and reinforce the unfortunate behaviors involved (thus, a human that perhaps wasn't contemplating feeding a wild dolphin, does so reactively when the dolphin comes up to them and appears to be requesting food).

Though many people think they are doing a kind thing by feeding wild dolphins, it is said that a fed dolphin will ultimately and regrettably become a dead dolphin, meaning that the dolphins will lose their natural competitive edge and be more likely to inevitably die sooner for one related reason or another.

This is reminiscent of those that go to our national parks and try to feed the wild deer. Signs are usually posted by the park rangers telling you that you should not feed the animals, but people do so anyway.

Each person doing so seems to think that a little bit of handed over morsel or other edible doesn't seem like much of an issue. They don't realize though that this act is done again and again by a multitude of visitors, thousands upon thousands over time, and gradually from the perspective of the deer it "teaches" them that humans have food and will readily provide food.

In many cases, the act of feeding a wild animal can get you into a lot of trouble with the law.

People seem to frequently assume that feeding a wild animal is indeed perhaps ill-advised, but they figure doing so is really at their own personal discretion.

Not so.

For example, per the U.S. Marine Mammal Protection Act, it is against the law to feed those wild dolphins in Florida, and it is illegal to hunt or kill the dolphins, all of which are acts that can lead to jail time and hefty fines.

The point or added twist then to the dolphin killings is that it could be that the wild dolphins had been fed by other humans from time-to-time, and it made the dolphins more complacent and actually eager to approach the reprobates that decided to kill them.

Had the dolphins been wary of humans, perhaps the mammals might have stayed far enough away to avoid being harmed or might not have made themselves visible to the killers.

To some degree, those that earlier had befriended the dolphins were inadvertently "training" the animals toward behavior that would likely undermine the survival of the mammals.

For those that feed wild animals, they think it is an act of kindness when in reality it is most likely an act of adverse consequences and undermines the animal's natural instincts.

Why bring up this topic?

Believe it or not, there is a similar kind of unintended adverse consequence that currently is possibly impacting the advent of AI-based true self-driving cars.

Say what?

Yes, let's consider this question: *Is human behavior around and toward true self-driving cars potentially undermining the realization of appropriate AI-based driving capabilities?*

Time to unpack the matter and see.

The Levels Of Self-Driving Cars

It is important to clarify what I mean when referring to true self-driving cars.

True self-driving cars are ones that the AI drives the car entirely on its own and there isn't any human assistance during the driving task.

These driverless vehicles are considered a Level 4 and Level 5, while a car that requires a human driver to co-share the driving effort is usually considered at a Level 2 or Level 3. The cars that co-share the driving task are described as being semi-autonomous, and typically contain a variety of automated add-on's that are referred to as ADAS (Advanced Driver-Assistance Systems).

There is not yet a true self-driving car at Level 5, which we don't yet even know if this will be possible to achieve, and nor how long it will take to get there.

Meanwhile, the Level 4 efforts are gradually trying to get some traction by undergoing very narrow and selective public roadway trials, though there is controversy over whether this testing should be allowed per se (we are all life-or-death guinea pigs in an experiment taking place on our highways and byways, some point out).

Since semi-autonomous cars require a human driver, the adoption of those types of cars won't be markedly different than driving conventional vehicles, so there's not much new per se to cover about them on this topic (though, as you'll see in a moment, the points next made are generally applicable).

For semi-autonomous cars, it is important that the public be forewarned about a disturbing aspect that's been arising lately, namely that in spite of those human drivers that keep posting videos of themselves falling asleep at the wheel of a Level 2 or Level 3 car, we all need to avoid being misled into believing that the driver can take away their attention from the driving task while driving a semi-autonomous car.

You are the responsible party for the driving actions of the vehicle, regardless of how much automation might be tossed into a Level 2 or Level 3.

Self-Driving Cars And Human Behavior

For Level 4 and Level 5 true self-driving vehicles, there won't be a human driver involved in the driving task.

All occupants will be passengers.

The AI is doing the driving.

One of the most important aspects of the AI driving system is that by-and-large it is being trained via Machine Learning (ML) and Deep Learning (DL).

In essence, rather than laboriously instructing the AI about how to drive a car step-by-step, the use of ML/DL involves feeding lots of data into a complex mathematical and computational algorithm that tries to find patterns and then utilize those patterns for subsequent actions.

I'll compare this to how a novice teenager learns to drive, though I don't want you to overly interpret the analogy and somehow believe that today's AI systems have human-thinking qualities (today's AI does not, despite whatever else you might have read or heard about such systems, so please don't be fooled or misled otherwise).

Do not anthropomorphize today's AI and assume that it has anything nearing human intelligence.

In any case, indulge a quick analogy, albeit with limitations.

For a novice teenage age driver, you might get into a car with them and explain inch-by-inch how to drive a car. Besides instructions on the use of the pedals and steering wheel, you might have the teenager start the car and take the vehicle for a drive in your local neighborhood.

As you do so, a caring parent is apt to say things like watch out for that pedestrian that appears to be nearing the street, or keep the car in the lane and don't veer out of your lane, or watch the car ahead of you that might at any moment hit its brakes.

Those are all explicit instructions about driving.

Another approach would be to have the teenager observe the roadway while driving, and potentially notice that sometimes pedestrians get near to the street, in which case it might be sensible to slow down and get ready to stop, just in case the person darts into the roadway.

In fact, for my kids, we used to play a game while they were younger that had them try to guess various roadway behaviors, doing so while sitting in the passenger seat. Though they weren't yet behind the wheel, by having made observations of the traffic situations this was allowing their minds to become ready-made drivers, being able to spot patterns in what happens around a driving car.

To a great extent, the AI-based true self-driving cars are using collected data about driving that becomes fodder for "learning" how to drive.

Feed-in lots of data, apply ML/DL, algorithmically spot patterns, and voila, you then potentially have guidance about how to drive a car.

One qualm about this approach is whether the AI is figuring out the right or correct ways to drive, plus if the data is rather homogenous it might not have unusual driving circumstances and thus there's no pattern to be formulated for what is referred to as "edge cases" (those are rare or less commonly encountered cases).

What in the world does this have to do with wild dolphins, you might be wondering?

Here's the connection.

Suppose that pedestrians upon seeing a self-driving car coming down the street are reactive in a manner unlike how they normally react to human-driven cars.

For example, in some areas, pedestrians opt to stay clear of the driverless cars that are being tried out on their neighborhood and downtown streets.

The logic seems to be that the self-driving cars are "special" and worthy of gawking at, but that you don't want to disturb the vehicle or upset whatever is taking place (and, admittedly, a bit of fear might be involved too, being rightfully wary of what the darned thing is going to do).

In contrast, for human-driven cars, those same pedestrians are oftentimes willing to play chicken with the drivers, stepping off the curb and daring the driver to proceed. In some cities, human drivers will accede to a jaywalker, while in other cities it becomes a do-or-die challenge as to whether the human gets across the street before the maddened car driver runs them over (a veritable game of Frogger).

Let's tie this back to the manner in which someone or something learn to drive.

If you were driving a car and never had any pedestrian that had tried to leap off the curb and dart into traffic, what might you "learn" about driving?

You could interpret this overarching pedestrian behavior to imply that you don't need to worry about pedestrians coming into your way. The lack of pedestrians that are willing to challenge the car is therefore inadvertently setting a pattern or tone of driving that you have an expectation of no pedestrian wackiness.

In a manner of speaking, the "kindness" of the pedestrians that are purposely holding back and not challenging a driverless car is essentially allowing the AI to "learn" that pedestrians are passive and not a likely threat to the driving act.

You could liken this to "training" wild dolphins by those that "befriend" the mammals and inadvertently undermining what the animals should actually know about the real-world.

Of course, we know what kind of adverse outcomes can befall the dolphins, so it would be useful to consider the kind of adverse outcomes that could befall AI self-driving cars.

Ponder the matter.

What might happen when a pedestrian suddenly and unexpectedly opts to run into the street and in front of an oncoming self-driving car?

The AI is likely to try and come to a halt, though it is conceivable that it will be caught somewhat off-guard and not be prepared to halt as soon as it could have otherwise accomplished. Without having built up a predictive expectation of such pedestrian behavior, the AI might be reliant predominantly on the sensors of the vehicle that happen to detect the pedestrian once they are already in the middle of the street.

It might be too late to come to a stop in time.

Had instead the AI been predicting that the pedestrian was likely to come into the street, it could have already begun to slow down or assess other means of avoiding the pedestrian.

Do not misunderstand and somehow assume that I'm suggesting the AI wouldn't likely try to come to a stop. The odds are that the overall AI system would try to do so.

The key in this example is that the AI might either not be anticipating what's going to happen or has no base of patterns to do so because the data used for ML/DL was without sufficient instances thereof.

When we humans drive, we anticipate the future. We don't just drive by whatever happens to come in front of the car. Most of us, at least those driving sensibly, scan back-and-forth, looking for a pedestrian that might come into traffic, or a dog that's running loose and might run in front of the car, or a tree that's ready to fall onto the roadway.

If AI-based true self-driving cars are going to drive at least as well as humans, there is a need to have a predictive quality that can anticipate what might happen, and then start on a timely basis to prepare for that potential action in-advance of the action itself playing out.

Pedestrians that are purposely avoiding a self-driving car rolling down the street are potentially undermining the adaptation of driving behaviors that we would want the AI to imbue.

Conclusion

Some smarmy pedestrian is going to read this and in a distorted manner think that I am suggesting that you ought to jump in front of an oncoming driverless car, as though that's a better way to train the AI.

No, that's plain stupid.

On a related matter, there are some that are pranking driverless cars, whereby they intentionally try to mess around with the AI system by doing something rash toward a self-driving car.

The most notable are those that while driving in traffic and upon spotting a driverless car, they maneuver to get in front of the self-driving car and then hit their brakes.

Apparently, those nutty drivers believe its fun and challenging to see what happens to the self-driving car when they pull these kinds of dangerous stunts. They also are seemingly too obtuse to realize that doing this to any driver, whether another human-driven car or a self-driving car, consists of an illegal driving act on their part and one that can have a terrible outcome for all parties.

Do not play pranks on self-driving cars.

The key to making sure that the AI driving systems are capable drivers consists of the AI developers and self-driving tech makers ensuring that the use of ML/DL is being undertaken in a sound manner.

As I've exhorted repeatedly, ML/DL for driverless cars can inadvertently become imbued with various biases as a result of the data being used to train them.

We rightfully should expect that those crafting these AI systems should be scrutinizing the data and also the patterns being surfaced, doing so to ensure that the data is representative and that the discovered patterns are sensible.

Today's AI systems do not have any robust form of common-sense reasoning and thus put aside any false assumption that magically the AI will realize that what it is doing is somehow wrong or inappropriate.

The act of learning is a lot more sophisticated than we generally give credit for.

As the sad tale of the wild dolphins illustrates, sometimes what is learned does not bode well.

Automakers and self-driving tech developers would be wise to keep those dolphins in mind, serving as a reminder that AI "learning" needs human guidance and must be done in a manner befitting the survival of us all, especially when dealing with multi-ton vehicles being allowed to rove on our busy and human-inhabited highways and byways.

CHAPTER 10

ANALYSIS OF AI IN GOVERNMENT REPORT

CHAPTER 10
ANALYSIS OF AI IN GOVERNMENT REPORT

One of the most frequently asked questions that I get at industry conferences is how far along the federal government has progressed in embracing AI.

Why does this question come up?

Some ask because they fervently believe that the government could do a much better job of providing agency services and likely perform its myriad of tasks more effectively by adopting the latest in AI technologies.

Others ask due to the concern that AI might be adopted in ways that could allow hastened governmental overreach and spur the potential of a dystopian society to arise via Big Brother algorithmic systems.

For all of those interested and inquisitive parties, your wish to discover what the government is doing about AI has been granted via a newly released report entitled *"Government by Algorithm: Artificial Intelligence in Federal Administrative Agencies."*

It's a hefty sized report that carefully and thoughtfully has examined the latest status of AI adoption by various federal entities, noting that indeed AI is getting traction, though unlike other such reports that merely offer bland lists of what's taking place, this report offers a deeper analysis of how the public will be impacted and opens the gate for well-needed public debate and further inquiry.

For example, as rightfully and outspokenly stated in the analysis, there are significant accountability challenges posed by many of these AI systems that our government is rapidly embracing.

How so?

At times, government agencies are apt to toss AI technology into the mix and do so without giving due consideration to the legal norms of transparency (of course, private industry is apt to make the same misstep too).

As I've repeatedly exhorted about the advent of Machine Learning (ML) and Deep Learning (DL), a predominantly data-based approach to AI, developers frequently rush ahead without considering how the resultant AI system might silently contain inherent biases and ultimately produce outcomes that are discriminatory (such as containing racial biases).

This is why organizations need to ensure that they proceed down the AI toolkit path in a measured manner, especially including a range of expertise as they do so, and encompass not just AI developers but also astute data scientists, professional ethicists, and others that can help to ascertain that an AI system is fair and balanced.

Fortunately, this report was put together by a wide-ranging team of specialists that included notable legal scholars, computer scientists, social scientists, and other experts, and was commissioned by the ACUS (Administrative Conference of the United States).

The ACUS is an independent nonpartisan federal agency that strives to aid the public and the government by identifying and promulgating improvements in how the government functions.

Typically, the ACUS undertakes in-depth analyses of the current state of the federal government and then produces a set of recommendations that are provided to Congress, the Executive branch, and the Judiciary about how to make improvements for the betterment of us all.

The four primary authors of this AI-focused report consisted of Professor David Engstrom of Stanford University, Professor Daniel Ho of Stanford University, Professor Catherine Sharkey of NYU, and Dr. Mariano-Florentino Cuellar currently a Justice on the Supreme Court of California and a Visiting Professor at Stanford University.

I met with Dr. David Engstrom and Dr. Daniel Ho and attended a public briefing about the report that they gave at Stanford as part of the exemplary *AI For Good* seminar series (link here) which explores how AI can be of benefit to society (undertaken by Stanford's Institute for Computational & Mathematical Engineering or ICME).

Readers might also find of great interest the Stanford Institute for Human-Centered Artificial Intelligence or HAI, which is an interdisciplinary hub for those seeking to better understand and shape the direction of AI toward enhancing the human condition.

See the 1-hour seminar YouTube video of Professor Engstrom and Professor Ho discussing the topic of AI for government and presenting the key findings of the report.

Some Details About the Report Scope

It is always important to be aware of the scope of any analysis, which therefore establishes a sense of context and enables the results to be appropriately interpreted and extrapolated from.

Overall, the report examines the largest 142 federal agencies (the metric for largeness consisted of the number of full-time equivalent employees).

Having started with a comprehensive list of 300 agencies via the ACUS Sourcebook, those agencies with less than 400 employees were culled from consideration for this specific study. This makes sense to do, providing a pragmatic scope to the study, aimed at understanding what the largest agencies are doing and are likely also the agencies that are bound to impact the most people.

Additionally, any active military and intelligence-related government entities were also removed from consideration (it would have been likely prohibitive to try and find out how such agencies are using AI due to the need for secrecy by those entities).

The data collection effort took place principally in the first eight months of last year, thus it is a snapshot in time, and of course, the agencies are continually in flux as to their ongoing AI efforts.

Overall, the analysis was based on publicly available or accessible info, and the intent was to surface AI ML/DL use cases that pertained to core agency activities by the government (in other words, there could be and probably likely are other *tangential* AI systems being developed and fielded).

Those of you that might be inspired to do a similar or follow-up study could potentially take a look at those agencies that have less than 400 employees.

Why do so?

On the one hand, you might assume that those agencies are perhaps too small to have the resources to craft an AI system, thus there would seem to be little value in exploring their use of AI (your research could end-up being the empty set).

But, it could also be that those agencies are the most in need of AI systems, perhaps due to being understaffed by labor and ergo unable to adequately achieve their services goals, while the use of properly devised AI could be a viable means by which they could ensure being responsive to public needs.

As such, what sometimes happens is that the most-strapped agencies put together AI-based systems, doing so on a shoestring budget and using duct tape, albeit in a genuine attempt to overcome their limited staffing.

Though this is perhaps to be applauded by those agencies, it also raises the specter that they could have very flimsy and off-the-cuff AI systems that despite being well-intended are going to ultimately be ill-advised for use.

Often, these AI systems become outdated and take on a zombie-like existence of continuing to be used though they have woefully drifted out-of-date and need to be either recrafted or summarily put aside (trying to drive a stake through the heart of a zombie AI-system can be much harder to do then you think, it becomes an integral part of the administrative fabric and just won't go down, no matter how many shots you take at it).

Indeed, this brings up a worthwhile history lesson, aiming to learn from history lest we are tempted to repeat it (well, repeating those aspects that we'd just as soon have learned to avoid or avert).

We are currently in an era of AI that many refer to as the AI Spring.

Prior to the AI Spring, there was the AI Winter (a time during which AI was less revered and had fallen somewhat out-of-favor).

The days prior to the AI Winter were a heyday of excitement for AI and became known for the advent of expert systems, also called knowledge-based systems or symbolic-AI.

Essentially, the attempt to craft AI-based systems consisted of identifying the golden nuggets of knowledge that domain experts used in performing their day-to-day tasks, and then imparting those bits of wisdom into various machine-executable rules.

Turns out that many of those knowledge-based systems were arduous and costly to build, and likewise arduous and costly to maintain.

To a great extent, the difficulties had to do with getting human domain experts to readily identify the "rules" that they used to perform their tasks. Knowledge elicitation is a messy and stubborn thing to achieve, plus getting the derived knowledge to be packed into simplistic rules was equally onerous to undertake.

Nowadays, the focus has shifted toward Machine Learning and Deep Learning (some refer to this as sub-symbolic-AI, or non-symbolic-AI, or more simply databased-AI).

For those pursuing ML/DL, the beauty of doing so is that you "only" need to find data, though you need a lot of it, and you can then apply ML/DL models to identify patterns in the data and subsequently generate presumed appropriate outcomes based on the patterns so discovered.

So, a key downfall of the expert systems era was that you needed to get access to live humans that were experts, you needed to magically get them to divulge how they do their work, and you needed to shovel that knowledge into an automated system.

With many of today's ML/DL efforts, those developing such AI systems often say, hey, give me all your data, and I'll figure out what's what.

Voila, no need to get those domain experts that were busy anyway and at times difficult to deal with, and instead all you have to do is go behind-the-scenes and grab up tons of data.

Furthermore, whereas knowledge-based systems were tricky to use and few knew how to use one for building an expert system, in the case of ML/DL you can pretty much use any of today's extended statistical packages that have expanded to include many of the more popular ML/DL modeling techniques.

In short, the kind of developers that you need for ML/DL is available on a wider basis than the prior era, since anyone with a modicum of statistics wherewithal believes they can build ML/DL systems, and the tools to do so are more readily available, and since your focus is on data it can be done in the background and avoid having to interact with domain experts (those darned pesky humans!).

Unfortunately, the pendulum might be swinging too far.

Many of the ML/DL efforts that falter or fail can be traced to the aspect that the developers had no real understanding of the data per se.

Had they spent time with the domain experts that underlie the realm of the data, they would have been better able to know what elements of the data were sound and which portions were out-of-whack.

And, the barrier to entry into crafting ML/DL is a lot lower than it used to be for knowledge-based systems.

That's good in that it means you can make a foray into such AI without necessarily busting your budget, though it also can allow for the pursuit of ML/DL efforts that are either unwise, or lack in proper planning, or that are pushed out-the-door without sufficient checks-and-balances (such as needed transparency).

Another twist has to do with explainability.

In the case of expert systems, the "rules" were readily able to be reviewed and inspected, and to some degree, you could garner an "explanation" for why the AI system did whatever it was doing (aka, due to being "symbolic" oriented AI).

With much of today's ML/DL, there is an increasing outcry that the algorithmically discovered patterns in large-scale datasets are inscrutable, consisting only of mathematically complex and computationally arcane indications that do not lend themselves to being explainable in human-like everyday ways (a pure black-box approach).

That's the rub with sub-symbolic AI or non-symbolic AI, namely, it presumes that data is data, and you don't necessarily need to comprehend the symbolism or symbolic nature of what the data consists of and nor the symbolic meaning of the embedded patterns detected.

There is a rapidly growing pursuit of XAI, so-called explainable AI, seeking to be able to take ML/DL models and lift-up the raw numbers and mathematically derived patterns into something understandable for human consumption.

What does this history lesson tell us?

In short, there is a sobering path right now of ML/DL developers producing AI-based systems that are unable to be explained, and that likely contain hidden assumptions that are not readily known or surfaced, and the resulting ML/DL is producing choices and recommendations that cannot be adequately tested and assessed, plus the ML/DL model is bound to have corner cases or edge cases that render the AI-system brittle and subject to adverse outcomes.

Some believe that if the AI Spring doesn't clean up its act, we might be headed toward another AI Winter (a seasonal condition that admittedly does come around, time after time).

Meanwhile, those that see the glass as half-full rather than perhaps half-empty, tend to believe that arising from all this inscrutability will be the dawn of true AI and an emergence of a singularity at which these ML/DL will miraculously achieve sentience (though, apparently, we won't know why it happened, and we won't even be able to predict when it will happen).

Time will tell.

Interesting Snippets Of The Report

About half of the surveyed federal agencies expressed that they were active in some manner related to AI/ML (so indicated 64 of the 142 studied, amounting to 45% of the selected pool), ranging from exploring ML/DL use to preparing plans or already in the midst of having implemented such a system.

Example use cases examined include the TSA's efforts of using image recognition to scan passenger luggage for potential explosives and HUD's deployment of a prototype AI-based chatbot for public interaction in learning about the agency programs.

And so on.

One case study that especially caught my attention dovetails into the pursuit of Autonomous Vehicles (AV's), including self-driving cars and self-driving trucks being considered for use by the U.S. Postal Service (USPS).

The U.S. Postal Service makes use of hundreds of thousands of vehicles, a rather staggering sized fleet.

According to USPS stats, it delivered 146.4 billion mail pieces in 2018, a mail volume that is about half of the world's total volume of mail (yes, you read that correctly, in the U.S. we account for what amounts to 47% of the entire world's mail volume).

Approximately 1.4 billion miles are traveled by the USPS in the act of delivering our mail.

Imagine if the USPS used self-driving cars and trucks.

There are 497,157 career employees and another 137,290 non-career employees in the USPS (again, 2018 stats).

One question arises as to what degree those vehicles would be zero-occupant versus human-occupant uses.

Presumably, there would be a huge labor savings if the driverless vehicles did not require a human, though of course there are (at least) two purposes for a human in the vehicle, one is to drive the vehicle and the other purpose is to complete the delivery act.

Assume that a self-driving car or driverless truck would allow the human to no longer need to drive the vehicle.

Could though a driverless car deal with the "last mile" or last few feet needed to make the mail delivery?

In other words, a driverless vehicle could arrive at a mail delivery location, and potentially make the delivery without a human needed to do so.

This is quite tricky and has yet to be solved.

If a mailbox is stationed at the curb and relatively easy to access, in theory, the self-driving vehicle could have some form of a robotic arm that might reach out and place the mail into the postal box.

For mailboxes that are at someone's doorstep or simply exists as a slot in their door, the manner of delivering the mail becomes much more complicated. A robot that can walk or otherwise go mobile might get out of the self-driving vehicle and make its way to the door (you've likely seen catchy online videos of recent robot prototypes doing as such for the major delivery firms such as FedEx, UPS, etc.).

Any discussion about how AI technology might aid in delivering mail needs to be tempered by the societal impacts involved.

For that half-a-million or so of USPS workers, what happens to them?

It's a thorny question.

Will the public accept the idea of a robot or robotic system coming up to their door to deliver mail?

And, a question that I've repeatedly raised involves the "roving eye" (my terminology, see **the link here**), regarding the data collected by self-driving vehicles while on-the-road.

Keep in mind that a self-driving vehicle is chockfull of video cameras, radar, LIDAR, and other sensory devices that are used by the on-board AI system to detect the driving scene and thus drive the vehicle accordingly.

Those sensory devices are collecting data about whatever is happening around the vehicle.

When a driverless car goes down your neighborhood street, it is essentially capturing all the activity taking place on your street. If you have self-driving vehicles routinely going on your street, you could stitch together the video and other sensory data to pretty much know who came out of their houses, when they did so, what they did, etc.

This is going to inevitably lead to a tremendous public debate about how that data shall be stored and utilized.

Having the USPS go driverless could lead to a massive privacy intrusion on a scale that few of us can imagine.

That's why this report is particularly worthwhile since the potential privacy implications and other societal ramifications of these kinds of AI adoption efforts by our government are given due consideration, while sadly many other AI in government reports tend to omit or give only short shrift to such aligned weighty aspects.

Conclusion

Those of you wanting to know what the federal government is doing about adopting AI ought to take a close look at this new report and ponder carefully where things are, along with where we might be heading.

You'll find plenty of evidence to support whichever viewpoint you might already have embraced, whether you are in the camp that sees AI as a heroic harbinger of better governmental services, or if you are in the camp that sees doom-and-gloom and villainous AI on the horizon.

Sometimes people tell me that there's nothing that can be done about an impending "AI takeover" and we might as well resign ourselves to a fate of being monitored and led by machines.

I don't buy into that kind of fatalism.

We are the makers of the machines and need to take into account the world that we are inexorably creating.

Step into the waters with the rest of us and join in steering AI toward a future that will hopefully mitigate or reduce the foulness and will illuminate and promulgate goodness for humanity.

I claim we make our own destiny on this.

CHAPTER 11

MOBILITY FRENZY AND AI SELF-DRIVING CARS

CHAPTER 11

MOBILITY FRENZY AND
AI SELF-DRIVING CARS

A colleague the other day drove over to a local grocery store to grab some holiday pies for the office, and then he drove about a half block's distance to get an Eggnog Latte at his favorite coffee shop.

There's nothing perhaps especially remarkable about this errand, other than the fact that rather than walking the half-block to get to the coffee shop from the grocery, he instead opted to use his car.

Why not simply walk over to the coffee shop, get the desired beverage, and scoot back to his car, gaining a little bit of exercise in the process to overcome the hefty calories of the latte and ultimately from consuming some of the pies later on in the day?

You might assume that foul weather prompted him to use his car for the half-block coffee quest.

Nope, there wasn't any rain, no snow, no inclement weather of any kind.

Maybe he had a bad leg or might be tired from carrying the pies out of the grocery store?

Nope, he's in perfectly good health and was readily capable of strutting the half-block distance.

Here in California, we are known for our car culture and devotion to using our automobiles for the smallest of distances.

Our motto seems to be that you'd be foolhardy to walk when you have a car that can get you to your desired destination, regardless of the distance involved.

Numerous publicly stated concerns have been raised about this kind of mindset.

Driving a car when you could have walked is tantamount to producing excess pollution that could have been otherwise avoided.

The driving act also causes the consumption of fuel, along with added wear-and-tear on the car and the roadway infrastructure, all of which seem unnecessary for short walkable trips.

And don't bring up the obesity topic and how valuable walking can be to your welfare, it's a point that might bring forth fisticuffs from some drivers that believe fervently in using their car to drive anyplace and all places, whenever they wish.

The odds are that my colleague might have walked from the grocery to the coffee shop if parking had not been so plentiful.

We all know how downright exasperating it can be to find a parking spot.

The angst of moving his car from the grocery store to the coffee shop would have been overwhelming to him if he had to drive around and around for fifteen minutes to find another place to park. The prospective pain of the parking chore would have been greater than the toss-in-the-towel walking chore, and his mental calculation would be to hoof it on foot.

Suppose that parking never became a problem again.

Suppose that using a car to go a half-block distance was always readily feasible.

In fact, suppose that you could use a car for any driving distance and could potentially even use a car to get from your house to a neighbor's home just down the street from you.

Some of us, maybe a lot of us, might become tempted to use cars a lot more than we do now.

In the United States, we go about 3.22 trillion miles per year via our cars. That's though based on various barriers or hurdles involved in opting to make use of a car.

Here's an intriguing question: *If we had true self-driving cars available, ready 24x7 to give you a lift, would we become more enamored of using cars and taking many more short trips?*

Think of the zillions of daily short trips that might be done via car use.

Add to that amount the ease of going longer distances than today you might not do, perhaps driving to see your grandma when you normally wouldn't feel up to the driving task.

The 3.22 trillion miles of car usage could jump dramatically.

It could rise by say 10% or 20%, or maybe double or triple in size.

It could generate an outsized mobility frenzy.

Let's unpack the matter and explore the implications of this seemingly uncapped explosion of car travel.

The Levels Of Self-Driving Cars

It is important to clarify what I mean when referring to true self-driving cars.

True self-driving cars are ones that the AI drives the car entirely on its own and there isn't any human assistance during the driving task.

These driverless cars are considered a Level 4 and Level 5, while a car that requires a human driver to co-share the driving effort is usually considered at a Level 2 or Level 3. The cars that co-share the driving task are described as being semi-autonomous, and typically contain a variety of automated add-ons that are referred to as ADAS (Advanced Driver-Assistance Systems).

There is not yet a true self-driving car at Level 5, which we don't yet even know if this will be possible to achieve, and nor how long it will take to get there.

Meanwhile, the Level 4 efforts are gradually trying to get some traction by undergoing very narrow and selective public roadway trials, though there is controversy over whether this testing should be allowed per se (we are all life-or-death guinea pigs in an experiment taking place on our highways and byways, some point out).

Since semi-autonomous cars require a human driver, the adoption of those types of cars won't be markedly different than driving conventional cars, so it's unlikely to have much of an impact on how many miles we opt to travel.

For semi-autonomous cars, it is equally important that I mention a disturbing aspect that's been arising, namely that in spite of those human drivers that keep posting videos of themselves falling asleep at the wheel of a Level 2 or Level 3 car, we all need to avoid being misled into believing that the driver can take away their attention from the driving task while driving a semi-autonomous car.

You are the responsible party for the driving actions of the car, regardless of how much automation might be tossed into a Level 2 or Level 3.

Self-Driving Cars And Distances Traveled

For Level 4 and Level 5 true self-driving cars, there won't be a human driver involved in the driving task.

All occupants will be passengers.

For those of you that use ridesharing today, you'll be joined by millions upon millions of other Americans that will be doing the same, except there won't be a human driver behind the wheel anymore.

Similar to requesting a ridesharing trip of today, we will all merely consult our smartphone and request a lift. The nearest self-driving car will respond to your request and arrive to pick you up.

Some believe that we'll have so many self-driving cars on our roads that they'll be quick to reach you.

Furthermore, these driverless cars will be roaming and meandering constantly, awaiting the next request for a pick-up, and thus will be statistically close to you whenever you make a request for a ride.

Nobody is sure what the cost to use self-driving cars will be, but let's assume for the moment that the cost is less than today's human-driven ridesharing services. Indeed, assume that the cost is a lot lower, perhaps several times less than a human-driven alternative.

Let's put two and two together.

Ubiquitous driverless cars, ready to give you a lift, doing so at a minimal cost, and can whisk you to whatever destination you specify.

The AI that's driving the car won't berate you for going a half-block.

No need to carry on idle chitchat with the AI.

It's like going for a ride in a chauffeur-driven car, and you are in full command of saying where you want to go, without any backlash from the driver (the AI isn't going to whine or complain, though perhaps there will be a mode that you can activate if that's the kind of driving journey you relish).

This is going to spark induced demand on steroids.

Induced demand refers to suppressed demand for a product or service that can spring forth once that product or service becomes more readily available.

The classic example involves adding a new lane to an existing highway or freeway. We've all experienced the circumstance whereby the new lane doesn't end-up alleviating traffic.

Why not?

Because there is usually suppressed demand that comes out of the woodwork to fill-up the added capacity. People that before were unwilling to get onto the roadway due to the traffic congestion are bound to think that the added lane makes it viable to now do so, yet once they start to use the highway it ends-up with so much traffic that once again the lanes get jammed.

With the advent of driverless cars, and once the availability of using car travel enters a nearly friction-free mode, the logical next step is that people will use car travel abundantly.

All those short trips that might have been costly to take or might have required a lot of waiting time, you'll now be able to undertake those with ease.

In fact, some believe that self-driving cars could undermine micro-mobility too.

Micro-mobility is the use of electric scooters, shared bikes and electric skateboards, which today are gradually growing in popularity to go the "last mile" to your destination.

If a driverless car can take you directly to your final destination, no need to bother with some other travel option such as micro-mobility.

How far down this self-driving car rabbit hole might we go?

There could be the emergence of a new cultural norm that you always are expected to use a driverless car, and anyone dumb enough or stubborn enough to walk or ride a bike is considered an oddball or outcast.

Is this what we want?

Could it cause some adverse consequences and spiral out-of-control?

Mobility Frenzy Gets A Backlash

Well, it could be that we are sensible enough that we realize there isn't a need to always use a driverless car when some alternative option exists.

Even if driverless cars are an easy choice, our society might assert that we should still walk and ride our bikes and scooters.

Since driverless cars are predicted to reduce the number of annual deaths and injuries due to car accidents, people might be more open to riding bikes and scooters, plus pedestrians might be less worried about getting run over by a car.

Futuristic cities and downtown areas might ban any car traffic in their inner core area. Self-driving cars will get you to the outer ring of the inner core, and from that point, you'll need to walk or use a micro-mobility selection.

From a pollution perspective, using today's combustion engine cars is replete with lots of tailpipe emissions.

The odds are that self-driving cars will be EV's (Electrical Vehicles), partially due to the need to have such vast amounts of electrical power for the AI and on-board computer processors. As such, the increased use of driverless cars won't boost pollution on par with gasoline-powered cars.

Nonetheless, there is a carbon footprint associated with the electrical charging of EV's. We might become sensitive to how much electricity we are consuming by taking so many driverless car trips. This could cause people to think twice before using a self-driving car.

Conclusion

Keep in mind that we are assuming that self-driving cars will be priced so low on a ridesharing basis that everyone will readily be able to afford to use driverless cars.

It could be that the cost is not quite as low as assumed, in which case the cost becomes a mitigating factor to dampen the mobility frenzy.

Another key assumption is that driverless cars will be plentiful and roaming so that they are within a short distance of anyone requesting a ride.

My colleague that was at the grocery store would have likely walked to the coffee shop in a world of self-driving cars if the driverless car was going to take longer to reach him than the time it would take to just hoof it over on his own.

And, this future era of mobility-for-all is going to occur many decades from now, since we today have 250 million conventional cars and it will take many years to gradually mothball them and have a new stock of self-driving cars gradually become prevalent.

Are self-driving cars going to be our Utopia, or might it be a Dystopia in which people no longer walk or ride bikes and instead get into their mobility bubbles and hide from their fellow humans while making the shortest of trips?

The frenzy would be of our own making, and hopefully, we could also deal with shaping it to ensure that we are still a society of people and walking, though I'm sure that some will still claim that walking is overrated.

APPENDIX

APPENDIX A

TEACHING WITH THIS MATERIAL

The material in this book can be readily used either as a supplemental to other content for a class, or it can also be used as a core set of textbook material for a specialized class. Classes where this material is most likely used include any classes at the college or university level that want to augment the class by offering thought provoking and educational essays about AI and self-driving cars.

In particular, here are some aspects for class use:

o   Computer Science. Studying AI, autonomous vehicles, etc.

o   Business. Exploring technology and it adoption for business.

o   Sociology. Sociological views on the adoption and advancement of technology.

Specialized classes at the undergraduate and graduate level can also make use of this material.

For each chapter, consider whether you think the chapter provides material relevant to your course topic. There is plenty of opportunity to get the students thinking about the topic and force them to decide whether they agree or disagree with the points offered and positions taken. I would also encourage you to have the students do additional research beyond the chapter material presented (I provide next some suggested assignments they can do).

RESEARCH ASSIGNMENTS ON THESE TOPICS

Your students can find background material on these topics, doing so in various business and technical publications. I list below the top ranked AI related journals. For business publications, I would suggest the usual culprits such as the Harvard Business Review, Forbes, Fortune, WSJ, and the like.

Here are some suggestions of homework or projects that you could assign to students:

a) <u>Assignment for foundational AI research topic</u>: Research and prepare a paper and a presentation on a specific aspect of Deep AI, Machine Learning, ANN, etc. The paper should cite at least 3 reputable sources. Compare and contrast to what has been stated in this book.

b) <u>Assignment for the Self-Driving Car topic</u>: Research and prepare a paper and Self-Driving Cars. Cite at least 3 reputable sources and analyze the characterizations. Compare and contrast to what has been stated in this book.

c) <u>Assignment for a Business topic</u>: Research and prepare a paper and a presentation on businesses and advanced technology. What is hot, and what is not? Cite at least 3 reputable sources. Compare and contrast to the depictions in this book.

d) <u>Assignment to do a Startup:</u> Have the students prepare a paper about how they might startup a business in this realm. They must submit a sound Business Plan for the startup. They could also be asked to present their Business Plan and so should also have a presentation deck to coincide with it.

You can certainly adjust the aforementioned assignments to fit to your particular needs and the class structure. You'll notice that I ask for 3 reputable cited sources for the paper writing based assignments. I usually steer students toward "reputable" publications, since otherwise they will cite some oddball source that has no credentials other than that they happened to write something and post it onto the Internet. You can define "reputable" in whatever way you prefer, for example some faculty think Wikipedia is not reputable while others believe it is reputable and allow students to cite it.

The reason that I usually ask for at least 3 citations is that if the student only does one or two citations they usually settle on whatever they happened to find the fastest. By requiring three citations, it usually seems to force them to look around, explore, and end-up probably finding five or more, and then whittling it down to 3 that they will actually use.

I have not specified the length of their papers, and leave that to you to tell the students what you prefer. For each of those assignments, you could end-up with a short one to two pager, or you could do a dissertation length paper. Base the length on whatever best fits for your class, and the credit amount of the assignment within the context of the other grading metrics you'll be using for the class.

I mention in the assignments that they are to do a paper and prepare a presentation. I usually try to get students to present their work. This is a good practice for what they will do in the business world. Most of the time, they will be required to prepare an analysis and present it. If you don't have the class time or inclination to have the students present, then you can of course cut out the aspect of them putting together a presentation.

If you want to point students toward highly ranked journals in AI, here's a list of the top journals as reported by *various citation counts sources* (this list changes year to year):

- Communications of the ACM
- Artificial Intelligence
- Cognitive Science
- IEEE Transactions on Pattern Analysis and Machine Intelligence
- Foundations and Trends in Machine Learning
- Journal of Memory and Language
- Cognitive Psychology
- Neural Networks
- IEEE Transactions on Neural Networks and Learning Systems
- IEEE Intelligent Systems
- Knowledge-based Systems

GUIDE TO USING THE CHAPTERS

For each of the chapters, I provide next some various ways to use the chapter material. You can assign the tasks as individual homework assignments, or the tasks can be used with team projects for the class. You can easily layout a series of assignments, such as indicating that the students are to do item "a" below for say Chapter 1, then "b" for the next chapter of the book, and so on.

a) What is the main point of the chapter and describe in your own words the significance of the topic,

b) Identify at least two aspects in the chapter that you agree with, and support your concurrence by providing at least one other outside researched item as support; make sure to explain your basis for disagreeing with the aspects,

c) Identify at least two aspects in the chapter that you disagree with, and support your disagreement by providing at least one other outside researched item as support; make sure to explain your basis for disagreeing with the aspects,

d) Find an aspect that was not covered in the chapter, doing so by conducting outside research, and then explain how that aspect ties into the chapter and what significance it brings to the topic,

e) Interview a specialist in industry about the topic of the chapter, collect from them their thoughts and opinions, and readdress the chapter by citing your source and how they compared and contrasted to the material,

f) Interview a relevant academic professor or researcher in a college or university about the topic of the chapter, collect from them their thoughts and opinions, and readdress the chapter by citing your source and how they compared and contrasted to the material,

g) Try to update a chapter by finding out the latest on the topic, and ascertain whether the issue or topic has now been solved or whether it is still being addressed, explain what you come up with.

The above are all ways in which you can get the students of your class involved in considering the material of a given chapter. You could mix things up by having one of those above assignments per each week, covering the chapters over the course of the semester or quarter.

As a reminder, here are the chapters of the book and you can select whichever chapters you find most valued for your particular class:

Chapter Title

1   Eliot Framework for AI Self-Driving Cars

2   Russian Values and AI Self-Driving Cars

3   Friendships Uplift and AI Self-Driving Cars

4   Dogs Driving and AI Self-Driving Cars

5   Hypodermic Needles and AI Self-Driving Cars

6   Sharing Self-Driving Tech Is Not Likely

7   Uber Driver "Kidnapper" Is Self-Driving Car Lesson

8   Gender Driving Biases In AI Self-Driving Cars

9   Slain Befriended Dolphins Are Self-Driving Car Lesson

10   Analysis Of AI In Government Report

11   Mobility Frenzy and AI Self-Driving Cars

<u>Companion Book By This Author</u>

Advances in AI and Autonomous Vehicles: Cybernetic Self-Driving Cars

*Practical Advances in Artificial Intelligence (AI)
and Machine Learning*

by

Dr. Lance B. Eliot, MBA, PhD

<u>Chapter Title</u>

1 Genetic Algorithms for Self-Driving Cars

2 Blockchain for Self-Driving Cars

3 Machine Learning and Data for Self-Driving Cars

4 Edge Problems at Core of True Self-Driving Cars

5 Solving the Roundabout Traversal Problem for SD Cars

6 Parallel Parking Mindless Task for SD Cars: Step It Up

7 Caveats of Open Source for Self-Driving Cars

8 Catastrophic Cyber Hacking of Self-Driving Cars

9 Conspicuity for Self-Driving Cars

10 Accident Scene Traversal for Self-Driving Cars

11 Emergency Vehicle Awareness for Self-Driving Cars

12 Are Left Turns Right for Self-Driving Cars

13 Going Blind: When Sensors Fail on Self-Driving Cars

14 Roadway Debris Cognition for Self-Driving Cars

15 Avoiding Pedestrian Roadkill by Self-Driving Cars

16 When Accidents Happen to Self-Driving Cars

17 Illegal Driving for Self-Driving Cars

18 Making AI Sense of Road Signs

19 Parking Your Car the AI Way

20 Not Fast Enough: Human Factors in Self-Driving Cars

21 State of Government Reporting on Self-Driving Cars

22 The Head Nod Problem for Self-Driving Cars

23 CES Reveals Self-Driving Car Differences

This title is available via Amazon and other book sellers

Companion Book By This Author

Self-Driving Cars:
"The Mother of All AI Projects"

by Dr. Lance B. Eliot, MBA, PhD

Chapter Title

1 Grand Convergence Explains Rise of Self-Driving Cars

2 Here is Why We Need to Call Them Self-Driving Cars

3 Richter Scale for Levels of Self-Driving Cars

4 LIDAR as Secret Sauce for Self-Driving Cars

5 Pied Piper Approach to SD Car-Following

6 Sizzle Reel Trickery for AI Self-Driving Car Hype

7 Roller Coaster Public Perception of Self-Driving Cars

8 Brainless Self-Driving Shuttles Not Same as SD Cars

9 First Salvo Class Action Lawsuits for Defective SD Cars

10 AI Fake News About Self-Driving Cars

11 Rancorous Ranking of Self-Driving Cars

12 Product Liability for Self-Driving Cars

13 Humans Colliding with Self-Driving Cars

14 Elderly Boon or Bust for Self-Driving Cars

15 Simulations for Self-Driving Cars: Machine Learning

16 DUI Drunk Driving by Self-Driving Cars

17 Ten Human-Driving Foibles: Deep Learning

18 Art of Defensive Driving is Key to Self-Driving Cars

19 Cyclops Approach to AI Self-Driving Cars is Myopic

20 Steering Wheel Gets Self-Driving Car Attention

21 Remote Piloting is a Self-Driving Car Crutch

22 Self-Driving Cars: Zero Fatalities, Zero Chance

23 Goldrush: Self-Driving Car Lawsuit Bonanza Ahead

24 Road Trip Trickery for Self-Driving Trucks and Cars

25 Ethically Ambiguous Self-Driving Car

This title is available via Amazon and other book sellers

Companion Book By This Author
Innovation and Thought Leadership on Self-Driving Driverless Cars
by Dr. Lance B. Eliot, MBA, PhD

Chapter Title

1 Sensor Fusion for Self-Driving Cars

2 Street Scene Free Space Detection Self-Driving Cars

3 Self-Awareness for Self-Driving Cars

4 Cartographic Trade-offs for Self-Driving Cars

5 Toll Road Traversal for Self-Driving Cars

6 Predictive Scenario Modeling for Self-Driving Cars

7 Selfishness for Self-Driving Cars

8 Leap Frog Driving for Self-Driving Cars

9 Proprioceptive IMU's for Self-Driving Cars

10 Robojacking of Self-Driving Cars

11 Self-Driving Car Moonshot and Mother of AI Projects

12 Marketing of Self-Driving Cars

13 Are Airplane Autopilots Same as Self-Driving Cars

14 Savvy Self-Driving Car Regulators: Marc Berman

15 Event Data Recorders (EDR) for Self-Driving Cars

16 Looking Behind You for Self-Driving Cars

17 In-Car Voice Commands NLP for Self-Driving Cars

18 When Self-Driving Cars Get Pulled Over by a Cop

19 Brainjacking Neuroprosthetus Self-Driving Cars

This title is available via Amazon and other book sellers

Companion Book By This Author

New Advances in AI Autonomous Driverless Cars Self-Driving Cars

by Dr. Lance B. Eliot, MBA, PhD

Chapter Title

1 Eliot Framework for AI Self-Driving Cars

2 Self-Driving Cars Learning from Self-Driving Cars

3 Imitation as Deep Learning for Self-Driving Cars

4 Assessing Federal Regulations for Self-Driving Cars

5 Bandwagon Effect for Self-Driving Cars

6 AI Backdoor Security Holes for Self-Driving Cars

7 Debiasing of AI for Self-Driving Cars

8 Algorithmic Transparency for Self-Driving Cars

9 Motorcycle Disentanglement for Self-Driving Cars

10 Graceful Degradation Handling of Self-Driving Cars

11 AI for Home Garage Parking of Self-Driving Cars

12 Motivational AI Irrationality for Self-Driving Cars

13 Curiosity as Cognition for Self-Driving Cars

14 Automotive Recalls of Self-Driving Cars

15 Internationalizing AI for Self-Driving Cars

16 Sleeping as AI Mechanism for Self-Driving Cars

17 Car Insurance Scams and Self-Driving Cars

18 U-Turn Traversal AI for Self-Driving Cars

19 Software Neglect for Self-Driving Cars

This title is available via Amazon and other book sellers

Companion Book By This Author
Introduction to
Driverless Self-Driving Cars
by Dr. Lance B. Eliot, MBA, PhD

Chapter Title

1 Self-Driving Car Moonshot: Mother of All AI Projects
2 Grand Convergence Leads to Self-Driving Cars
3 Why They Should Be Called Self-Driving Cars
4 Richter Scale for Self-Driving Car Levels
5 LIDAR for Self-Driving Cars
6 Overall Framework for Self-Driving Cars
7 Sensor Fusion is Key for Self-Driving Cars
8 Humans Not Fast Enough for Self-Driving Cars
9 Solving Edge Problems of Self-Driving Cars
10 Graceful Degradation for Faltering Self-Driving Cars
11 Genetic Algorithms for Self-Driving Cars
12 Blockchain for Self-Driving Cars
13 Machine Learning and Data for Self-Driving Cars
14 Cyber-Hacking of Self-Driving Cars
15 Sensor Failures in Self-Driving Cars
16 When Accidents Happen to Self-Driving Cars
17 Backdoor Security Holes in Self-Driving Cars
18 Future Brainjacking for Self-Driving Cars
19 Internationalizing Self-Driving Cars
20 Are Airline Autopilots Same as Self-Driving Cars
21 Marketing of Self-Driving Cars
22 Fake News about Self-Driving Cars
23 Product Liability for Self-Driving Cars
24 Zero Fatalities Zero Chance for Self-Driving Cars
25 Road Trip Trickery for Self-Driving Cars
26 Ethical Issues of Self-Driving Cars
27 Ranking of Self-Driving Cars
28 Induced Demand Driven by Self-Driving Cars

This title is available via Amazon and other book sellers

Companion Book By This Author

Autonomous Vehicle Driverless
Self-Driving Cars and Artificial Intelligence

by Dr. Lance B. Eliot, MBA, PhD

Chapter Title

1   Eliot Framework for AI Self-Driving Cars

2   Rocket Man Drivers and AI Self-Driving Cars

3   Occam's Razor Crucial for AI Self-Driving Cars

4   Simultaneous Local/Map (SLAM) for Self-Driving Cars

5   Swarm Intelligence for AI Self-Driving Cars

6   Biomimicry and Robomimicry for Self-Driving Cars

7   Deep Compression/Pruning for AI Self-Driving Cars

8   Extra-Scenery Perception for AI Self-Driving Cars

9   Invasive Curve and AI Self-Driving Cars

10 Normalization of Deviance and AI Self-Driving Cars

11 Groupthink Dilemma for AI Self-Driving Cars

12 Induced Demand Driven by AI Self-Driving Cars

13 Compressive Sensing for AI Self-Driving Cars

14 Neural Layer Explanations for AI Self-Driving Cars

15 Self-Adapting Resiliency for AI Self-Driving Cars

16 Prisoner's Dilemma and AI Self-Driving Cars

17 Turing Test and AI Self-Driving Cars

18 Support Vector Machines for AI Self-Driving Cars

19 "Expert Systems and AI Self-Driving Cars" by Michael Eliot

This title is available via Amazon and other book sellers

Companion Book By This Author

Transformative Artificial Intelligence Driverless Self-Driving Cars

by Dr. Lance B. Eliot, MBA, PhD

Chapter Title

1 Eliot Framework for AI Self-Driving Cars

2 Kinetosis Anti-Motion Sickness for Self-Driving Cars

3 Rain Driving for Self-Driving Cars

4 Edge Computing for Self-Driving Cars

5 Motorcycles as AI Self-Driving Vehicles

6 CAPTCHA Cyber-Hacking and Self-Driving Cars

7 Probabilistic Reasoning for Self-Driving Cars

8 Proving Grounds for Self-Driving Cars

9 Frankenstein and AI Self-Driving Cars

10 Omnipresence for Self-Driving Cars

11 Looking Behind You for Self-Driving Cars

12 Over-The-Air (OTA) Updating for Self-Driving Cars

13 Snow Driving for Self-Driving Cars

14 Human-Aided Training for Self-Driving Cars

15 Privacy for Self-Driving Cars

16 Transduction Vulnerabilities for Self-Driving Cars

17 Conversations Computing and Self-Driving Cars

18 Flying Debris and Self-Driving Cars

19 Citizen AI for Self-Driving Cars

This title is available via Amazon and other book sellers

<u>Companion Book By This Author</u>

***Disruptive Artificial Intelligence
and Driverless Self-Driving Cars***

by Dr. Lance B. Eliot, MBA, PhD

<u>Chapter Title</u>

1   Eliot Framework for AI Self-Driving Cars

2   Maneuverability and Self-Driving Cars

3   Common Sense Reasoning and Self-Driving Cars

4   Cognition Timing and Self-Driving Cars

5   Speed Limits and Self-Driving Vehicles

6   Human Back-up Drivers and Self-Driving Cars

7   Forensic Analysis Uber and Self-Driving Cars

8   Power Consumption and Self-Driving Cars

9   Road Rage and Self-Driving Cars

10 Conspiracy Theories and Self-Driving Cars

11 Fear Landscape and Self-Driving Cars

12 Pre-Mortem and Self-Driving Cars

13 Kits and Self-Driving Cars

This title is available via Amazon and other book sellers

<u>Companion Book By This Author</u>

State-of-the-Art
AI Driverless Self-Driving Cars

by Dr. Lance B. Eliot, MBA, PhD

<u>Chapter Title</u>

1 Eliot Framework for AI Self-Driving Cars

2 Versioning and Self-Driving Cars

3 Towing and Self-Driving Cars

4 Driving Styles and Self-Driving Cars

5 Bicyclists and Self-Driving Vehicles

6 Back-up Cams and Self-Driving Cars

7 Traffic Mix and Self-Driving Cars

8 Hot-Car Deaths and Self-Driving Cars

9 Machine Learning Performance and Self-Driving Cars

10 Sensory Illusions and Self-Driving Cars

11 Federated Machine Learning and Self-Driving Cars

12 Irreproducibility and Self-Driving Cars

13 In-Car Deliveries and Self-Driving Cars

This title is available via Amazon and other book sellers

<u>Companion Book By This Author</u>

Top Trends in
AI Self-Driving Cars

by Dr. Lance B. Eliot, MBA, PhD

<u>Chapter Title</u>

1 Eliot Framework for AI Self-Driving Cars

2 Responsibility and Self-Driving Cars

3 Changing Lanes and Self-Driving Cars

4 Procrastination and Self-Driving Cars

5 NTSB Report and Tesla Car Crash

6 Start Over AI and Self-Driving Cars

7 Freezing Robot Problem and Self-Driving Cars

8 Canarying and Self-Driving Cars

9 Nighttime Driving and Self-Driving Cars

10 Zombie-Cars Taxes and Self-Driving Cars

11 Traffic Lights and Self-Driving Cars

12 Reverse Engineering and Self-Driving Cars

13 Singularity AI and Self-Driving Cars

This title is available via Amazon and other book sellers

Companion Book By This Author

AI Innovations and Self-Driving Cars

by Dr. Lance B. Eliot, MBA, PhD

Chapter Title

1   Eliot Framework for AI Self-Driving Cars

2   API's and Self-Driving Cars

3   Egocentric Designs and Self-Driving Cars

4   Family Road Trip and Self-Driving Cars

5   AI Developer Burnout and Tesla Car Crash

6   Stealing Secrets About Self-Driving Cars

7   Affordability and Self-Driving Cars

8   Crossing the Rubicon and Self-Driving Cars

9   Addicted to Self-Driving Cars

10 Ultrasonic Harm and Self-Driving Cars

11 Accidents Contagion and Self-Driving Cars

12 Non-Stop 24x7 and Self-Driving Cars

13 Human Life Spans and Self-Driving Cars

This title is available via Amazon and other book sellers

Companion Book By This Author

Crucial Advances for
AI Self-Driving Cars

by Dr. Lance B. Eliot, MBA, PhD

Chapter Title

1   Eliot Framework for AI Self-Driving Cars

2   Ensemble Learning and AI Self-Driving Cars

3   Ghost in AI Self-Driving Cars

4   Public Shaming of AI Self-Driving

5   Internet of Things (IoT) and AI Self-Driving Cars

6   Personal Rapid Transit (RPT) and Self-Driving Cars

7   Eventual Consistency and AI Self-Driving Cars

8   Mass Transit Future and AI Self-Driving Cars

9   Coopetition and AI Self-Driving Cars

10 Electric Vehicles (EVs) and AI Self-Driving Cars

11 Dangers of In-Motion AI Self-Driving Cars

12 Sports Cars and AI Self-Driving Cars

13 Game Theory and AI Self-Driving Cars

This title is available via Amazon and other book sellers

Companion Book By This Author

Sociotechnical Insights and AI Driverless Cars

by Dr. Lance B. Eliot, MBA, PhD

Chapter Title

1 Eliot Framework for AI Self-Driving Cars

2 Start-ups and AI Self-Driving Cars

3 Code Obfuscation and AI Self-Driving Cars

4 Hyperlanes and AI Self-Driving Cars

5 Passenger Panic Inside an AI Self-Driving Car

6 Tech Stockholm Syndrome and Self-Driving Cars

7 Paralysis and AI Self-Driving Cars

8 Ugly Zones and AI Self-Driving Cars

9 Ridesharing and AI Self-Driving Cars

10 Multi-Party Privacy and AI Self-Driving Cars

11 Chaff Bugs and AI Self-Driving Cars

12 Social Reciprocity and AI Self-Driving Cars

13 Pet Mode and AI Self-Driving Cars

This title is available via Amazon and other book sellers

Companion Book By This Author

Pioneering Advances for AI Driverless Cars

by Dr. Lance B. Eliot, MBA, PhD

Chapter Title

1 Eliot Framework for AI Self-Driving Cars

2 Boxes on Wheels and AI Self-Driving Cars

3 Clogs and AI Self-Driving Cars

4 Kids Communicating with AI Self-Driving Cars

5 Incident Awareness and AI Self-Driving Car

6 Emotion Recognition and Self-Driving Cars

7 Rear-End Collisions and AI Self-Driving Cars

8 Autonomous Nervous System and AI Self-Driving Cars

9 Height Warnings and AI Self-Driving Cars

10 Future Jobs and AI Self-Driving Cars

11 Car Wash and AI Self-Driving Cars

12 5G and AI Self-Driving Cars

13 Gen Z and AI Self-Driving Cars

This title is available via Amazon and other book sellers

Companion Book By This Author

Leading Edge Trends for AI Driverless Cars

by Dr. Lance B. Eliot, MBA, PhD

Chapter Title

1 Eliot Framework for AI Self-Driving Cars

2 Pranking and AI Self-Driving Cars

3 Drive-Thrus and AI Self-Driving Cars

4 Overworking on AI Self-Driving Cars

5 Sleeping Barber Problem and AI Self-Driving Cars

6 System Load Balancing and AI Self-Driving Cars

7 Virtual Spike Strips and AI Self-Driving Cars

8 Razzle Dazzle Camouflage and AI Self-Driving Cars

9 Rewilding of AI Self-Driving Cars

10 Brute Force Algorithms and AI Self-Driving Cars

11 Idle Moments and AI Self-Driving Cars

12 Hurricanes and AI Self-Driving Cars

13 Object Visual Transplants and AI Self-Driving Cars

This title is available via Amazon and other book sellers

Companion Book By This Author

The Cutting Edge of
AI Autonomous Cars

by Dr. Lance B. Eliot, MBA, PhD

Chapter Title

1   Eliot Framework for AI Self-Driving Cars

2   Driving Controls and AI Self-Driving Cars

3   Bug Bounty and AI Self-Driving Cars

4   Lane Splitting and AI Self-Driving Cars

5   Drunk Drivers versus AI Self-Driving Cars

6   Internal Naysayers and AI Self-Driving Cars

7   Debugging and AI Self-Driving Cars

8   Ethics Review Boards and AI Self-Driving Cars

9   Road Diets and AI Self-Driving Cars

10 Wrong Way Driving and AI Self-Driving Cars

11 World Safety Summit and AI Self-Driving Cars

This title is available via Amazon and other book sellers

Companion Book By This Author

The Next Wave of
AI Self-Driving Cars

by Dr. Lance B. Eliot, MBA, PhD

Chapter Title

1   Eliot Framework for AI Self-Driving Cars

2   Productivity and AI Self-Driving Cars

3   Blind Pedestrians and AI Self-Driving Cars

4   Fail-Safe AI and AI Self-Driving Cars

5   Anomaly Detection and AI Self-Driving Cars

6   Running Out of Gas and AI Self-Driving Cars

7   Deep Personalization and AI Self-Driving Cars

8   Reframing the Levels of AI Self-Driving Cars

9   Cryptojacking and AI Self-Driving Cars

This title is available via Amazon and other book sellers

Companion Book By This Author

Revolutionary Innovations of
AI Self-Driving Cars

by Dr. Lance B. Eliot, MBA, PhD

Chapter Title

1 Eliot Framework for AI Self-Driving Cars

2 Exascale Supercomputer and AI Self-Driving Cars

3 Superhuman AI and AI Self-Driving Cars

4 Olfactory e-Nose Sensors and AI Self-Driving Cars

5 Perpetual Computing and AI Self-Driving Cars

6 Byzantine Generals Problem and AI Self-Driving Cars

7 Driver Traffic Guardians and AI Self-Driving Cars

8 Anti-Gridlock Laws and AI Self-Driving Cars

9 Arguing Machines and AI Self-Driving Cars

This title is available via Amazon and other book sellers

<u>Companion Book By This Author</u>

AI Self-Driving Cars
Breakthroughs

by Dr. Lance B. Eliot, MBA, PhD

<u>Chapter Title</u>

1 Eliot Framework for AI Self-Driving Cars

2 Off-Roading and AI Self-Driving Cars

3 Paralleling Vehicles and AI Self-Driving Cars

4 Dementia Drivers and AI Self-Driving Cars

5 Augmented Realty (AR) and AI Self-Driving Cars

6 Sleeping Inside an AI Self-Driving Car

7 Prevalence Detection and AI Self-Driving Cars

8 Super-Intelligent AI and AI Self-Driving Cars

9 Car Caravans and AI Self-Driving Cars

This title is available via Amazon and other book sellers

<u>Companion Book By This Author</u>

Trailblazing Trends for
AI Self-Driving Cars

by Dr. Lance B. Eliot, MBA, PhD

<u>Chapter Title</u>

1   Eliot Framework for AI Self-Driving Cars

2   Strategic AI Metaphors and AI Self-Driving Cars

3   Emergency-Only AI and AI Self-Driving Cars

4   Animal Drawn Vehicles and AI Self-Driving Cars

5   Chess Play and AI Self-Driving Cars

6   Cobots Exoskeletons and AI Self-Driving Car

7   Economic Commodity and AI Self-Driving Cars

8   Road Racing and AI Self-Driving Cars

This title is available via Amazon and other book sellers

Companion Book By This Author

Ingenious Strides for
AI Driverless Cars

by Dr. Lance B. Eliot, MBA, PhD

Chapter Title

1 Eliot Framework for AI Self-Driving Cars

2 Plasticity and AI Self-Driving Cars

3 NIMBY vs. YIMBY and AI Self-Driving Cars

4 Top Trends for 2019 and AI Self-Driving Cars

5 Rural Areas and AI Self-Driving Cars

6 Self-Imposed Constraints and AI Self-Driving Car

7 Alien Limb Syndrome and AI Self-Driving Cars

8 Jaywalking and AI Self-Driving Cars

This title is available via Amazon and other book sellers

Companion Book By This Author

AI Self-Driving Cars
Inventiveness

by Dr. Lance B. Eliot, MBA, PhD

Chapter Title

1 Eliot Framework for AI Self-Driving Cars

2 Crumbling Infrastructure and AI Self-Driving Cars

3 e-Billboarding and AI Self-Driving Cars

4 Kinship and AI Self-Driving Cars

5 Machine-Child Learning and AI Self-Driving Cars

6 Baby-on-Board and AI Self-Driving Car

7 Cop Car Chases and AI Self-Driving Cars

8 One-Shot Learning and AI Self-Driving Cars

This title is available via Amazon and other book sellers

Companion Book By This Author

***Visionary Secrets of
AI Driverless Cars***

by Dr. Lance B. Eliot, MBA, PhD

Chapter Title

1   Eliot Framework for AI Self-Driving Cars

2   Seat Belts and AI Self-Driving Cars

3   Tiny EV's and AI Self-Driving Cars

4   Empathetic Computing and AI Self-Driving Cars

5   Ethics Global Variations and AI Self-Driving Cars

6   Computational Periscopy and AI Self-Driving Car

7   Superior Cognition and AI Self-Driving Cars

8   Amalgamating ODD's and AI Self-Driving Cars

This title is available via Amazon and other book sellers

Companion Book By This Author

Spearheading
AI Self-Driving Cars

by Dr. Lance B. Eliot, MBA, PhD

Chapter Title

1 Eliot Framework for AI Self-Driving Cars

2 Artificial Pain and AI Self-Driving Cars

3 Stop-and-Frisks and AI Self-Driving Cars

4 Cars Careening and AI Self-Driving Cars

5 Sounding Out Car Noises and AI Self-Driving Cars

6 No Speed Limit Autobahn and AI Self-Driving Car

7 Noble Cause Corruption and AI Self-Driving Cars

8 AI Rockstars and AI Self-Driving Cars

This title is available via Amazon and other book sellers

Companion Book By This Author

Spurring
AI Self-Driving Cars
by Dr. Lance B. Eliot, MBA, PhD

Chapter Title

1 Eliot Framework for AI Self-Driving Cars

2 Triune Brain Theory and AI Self-Driving Cars

3 Car Parts Thefts and AI Self-Driving Cars

4 Goto Fail Bug and AI Self-Driving Cars

5 Scrabble Understanding and AI Self-Driving Cars

6 Cognition Disorders and AI Self-Driving Car

7 Noise Pollution Abatement AI Self-Driving Cars

This title is available via Amazon and other book sellers

Companion Book By This Author

Avant-Garde
AI Driverless Cars

by Dr. Lance B. Eliot, MBA, PhD

Chapter Title

1   Eliot Framework for AI Self-Driving Cars

2   Linear Non-Threshold and AI Self-Driving Cars

3   Prediction Equation and AI Self-Driving Cars

4   Modular Autonomous Systems and AI Self-Driving Cars

5   Driver's Licensing and AI Self-Driving Cars

6   Offshoots and Spinoffs and AI Self-Driving Car

7   Depersonalization and AI Self-Driving Cars

This title is available via Amazon and other book sellers

Companion Book By This Author

AI Self-Driving Cars
Evolvement

by Dr. Lance B. Eliot, MBA, PhD

Chapter Title

1   Eliot Framework for AI Self-Driving Cars

2   Chief Safety Officers and AI Self-Driving Cars

3   Bounded Volumes and AI Self-Driving Cars

4   Micro-Movements Behaviors and AI Self-Driving Cars

5   Boeing 737 Aspects and AI Self-Driving Cars

6   Car Controls Commands and AI Self-Driving Car

7   Multi-Sensor Data Fusion and AI Self-Driving Cars

This title is available via Amazon and other book sellers

Companion Book By This Author

AI Driverless Cars
Chrysalis

by Dr. Lance B. Eliot, MBA, PhD

Chapter Title

1   Eliot Framework for AI Self-Driving Cars

2   Object Poses and AI Self-Driving Cars

3   Human In-The-Loop and AI Self-Driving Cars

4   Genius Shortage and AI Self-Driving Cars

5   Salvage Yards and AI Self-Driving Cars

6   Precision Scheduling and AI Self-Driving Car

7   Human Driving Extinction and AI Self-Driving Cars

This title is available via Amazon and other book sellers

Companion Book By This Author

Boosting
AI Autonomous Cars
by Dr. Lance B. Eliot, MBA, PhD

Chapter Title

1   Eliot Framework for AI Self-Driving Cars

2   Zero Knowledge Proofs and AI Self-Driving Cars

3   Active Shooter Response and AI Self-Driving Cars

4   Free Will and AI Self-Driving Cars

5   No Picture Yet of AI Self-Driving Cars

6   Boeing 737 Lessons and AI Self-Driving Cars

7   Preview Tesla FSD and AI Self-Driving Cars

8   LIDAR Industry and AI Self-Driving Cars

9   Uber IPO and AI Self-Driving Cars

10   Suing Automakers of AI Self-Driving Cars

11   Tesla Overarching FSD and AI Self-Driving Cars

12   Auto Repair Market and AI Self-Driving Cars

This title is available via Amazon and other book sellers

Companion Book By This Author

AI Self-Driving Cars
Trendsetting

by Dr. Lance B. Eliot, MBA, PhD

Chapter Title

1   Eliot Framework for AI Self-Driving Cars

2   OTA Myths and AI Self-Driving Cars

3   Surveys and AI Self-Driving Cars

4   Tech Spies and AI Self-Driving Cars

5   Anxieties and AI Self-Driving Cars

6   Achilles Heel and AI Self-Driving Cars

7   Kids Alone and AI Self-Driving Cars

8   Infrastructure and AI Self-Driving Cars

9   Distracted Driving and AI Self-Driving Cars

10   Human Drivers and AI Self-Driving Cars

11   Anti-LIDAR Stance and AI Self-Driving Cars

12   Autopilot Team and AI Self-Driving Cars

13   Rigged Videos and AI Self-Driving Cars

14   Stalled Cars and AI Self-Driving Cars

15   Princeton Summit and AI Self-Driving Cars

16   Brittleness and AI Self-Driving Cars

17   Mergers and AI Self-Driving Cars

This title is available via Amazon and other book sellers

Companion Book By This Author

AI Autonomous Cars
Forefront

by Dr. Lance B. Eliot, MBA, PhD

Chapter Title

1   Eliot Framework for AI Self-Driving Cars

2   Essential Stats and AI Self-Driving Cars

3   Stats Fallacies and AI Self-Driving Cars

4   Driver Bullies and AI Self-Driving Cars

5   Sunday Drives and AI Self-Driving Cars

6   Face Recog Bans and AI Self-Driving Cars

7   States On-The-Hook and AI Self-Driving Cars

8   Sensors Profiting and AI Self-Driving Cars

9   Unruly Riders and AI Self Driving Cars

10   Father's Day and AI Self-Driving Cars

11   Summons Feature and AI Self-Driving Cars

12   Libra Cryptocurrency and AI Self-Driving Cars

13   Systems Naming and AI Self-Driving Cars

14   Mid-Traffic Rendezvous and AI Self-Driving Cars

15   Pairing Drones and AI Self-Driving Cars

16   Lost Wallet Study and AI Self-Driving Cars

This title is available via Amazon and other book sellers

Companion Book By This Author

AI Autonomous Cars Emergence

by Dr. Lance B. Eliot, MBA, PhD

Chapter Title

1   Eliot Framework for AI Self-Driving Cars

2   Dropping Off Riders and AI Self-Driving Cars

3   Add-On Kits Drive.AI and AI Self-Driving Cars

4   Boeing 737 Emergency Flaw and AI Self-Driving Cars

5   Spinout Tesla Autopilot and AI Self-Driving Cars

6   Earthquakes and AI Self-Driving Cars

7   Ford Mobility Lab and AI Self-Driving Cars

8   Apollo 11 Error Code and AI Self-Driving Cars

9   Nuro Self-Driving Vehicle and AI Self-Driving Cars

10   Safety First (SaFAD) Aptiv and AI Self-Driving Cars

11   Brainjacking Neuralink and AI Self-Driving Cars

12   Storming Area 51 and AI Self-Driving Cars

13   Riding Inside An AI Self-Driving Car

14   ACES Acronym and AI Self-Driving Cars

15   Kids Bike Riding and AI Self-Driving Cars

16   LIDAR Not Doomed and AI Self-Driving Cars

This title is available via Amazon and other book sellers

Companion Book By This Author

AI Autonomous Cars Progress

by Dr. Lance B. Eliot, MBA, PhD

Chapter Title

1 Eliot Framework for AI Self-Driving Cars

2 Risk-O-Meters and AI Self-Driving Cars

3 Eroding Car Devotion and AI Self-Driving Cars

4 Drunk Driving Rises With Smart Cars

5 Driver's Difficulties and Smart Cars

6 Millennials Aren't As Car Crazed As Baby Boomers

7 Risks Of AI Self-Driving Cars

8 Major Phase Shift and AI Self-Driving Cars

9 Level 3 Tech Misgivings For Smart Cars

10 Presidential Debate Lessons and AI Self-Driving Cars

11 Cloud Breeches and AI Self-Driving Cars

12 The Moral Imperative and AI Self-Driving Cars

13 Freed Up Driver Time And AI Self-Driving Car

14 Deadliest Highways and AI Self-Driving Cars

15 Your Lyin' Eyes and AI Self-Driving Cars

16 Elon Musk Physics Mindset and AI Self-Driving Cars

This title is available via Amazon and other book sellers

Companion Book By This Author

AI Self-Driving Cars
Prognosis

by Dr. Lance B. Eliot, MBA, PhD

Chapter Title

1 Eliot Framework for AI Self-Driving Cars

2 Roadkill and AI Self-Driving Cars

3 Safe Driver Cities and AI Self-Driving Cars

4 Tailgate Parties and AI Self-Driving Cars

5 Tesla's AI Chips and AI Self-Driving Cars

6 Elites-Only and AI Self-Driving Cars

7 Four Year Lifecycle and AI Self-Driving Cars

8 Entrepreneurs and AI Self-Driving Cars

9 Autopilot Crash Lessons and AI Self-Driving Cars

10 U.N. Framework and AI Self-Driving Cars

11 Sports Cars and AI Self-Driving Cars

12 Railroad Crossings and AI Self-Driving Cars

13 Robots That Drive and AI Self-Driving Car

14 Smarts Over Speed and AI Self-Driving Cars

15 Havoc Ratings and AI Self-Driving Cars

16 Sex-on-Wheels and AI Self-Driving Cars

This title is available via Amazon and other book sellers

Companion Book By This Author

AI Self-Driving Cars
Momentum

by Dr. Lance B. Eliot, MBA, PhD

Chapter Title

1 Eliot Framework for AI Self-Driving Cars

2 Solving Loneliness and AI Self-Driving Cars

3 Headless Issues and AI Self-Driving Cars

4 Roaming Empty and AI Self-Driving Cars

5 Millennials Exodus and AI Self-Driving Cars

6 Recession Worries and AI Self-Driving Cars

7 Remote Operation Issues and AI Self-Driving Cars

8 Boomerang Kids and AI Self-Driving Cars

9 Waymo Coming To L.A. and AI Self-Driving Cars

10 Getting To Scale and AI Self-Driving Cars

11 Looking Alike and AI Self-Driving Cars

12 NOVA Documentary On AI Self-Driving Cars

13 Birthrate Changes and AI Self-Driving Cars

This title is available via Amazon and other book sellers

Lance B. Eliot

Companion Book By This Author

AI Self-Driving Cars
Headway

by Dr. Lance B. Eliot, MBA, PhD

Chapter Title

1   Eliot Framework for AI Self-Driving Cars

2   Germs Spreading and AI Self-Driving Cars

3   Carbon Footprint and AI Self-Driving Cars

4   Protestors Use Of AI Self-Driving Cars

5   Rogue Behavior and AI Self-Driving Cars

6   Using Human Drivers Versus AI Self-Driving Cars

7   Tesla Hodge-Podge On AI Self-Driving Cars

8   Solo Occupancy and AI Self-Driving Cars

9   Einstein's Twins Paradox and AI Self-Driving Cars

10   Nation-State Takeover Of AI Self-Driving Cars

11   Quantum Computers and AI Self-Driving Cars

12   Religious Revival And AI Self-Driving Cars

This title is available via Amazon and other book sellers

Companion Book By This Author

AI Self-Driving Cars
Vicissitude

by Dr. Lance B. Eliot, MBA, PhD

Chapter Title

1   Eliot Framework for AI Self-Driving Cars

2   Leaving A Tip and AI Self-Driving Cars

3   Digital Nudging and AI Self-Driving Cars

4   Carpool Lanes and AI Self-Driving Cars

5   Sleep Solving and AI Self-Driving Cars

6   Nostradamus and AI Self-Driving Cars

7   Advanced Driving and AI Self-Driving Cars

8   Cybertruck Windows Shattered Mystery

9   Artificial Stupidity and AI Self-Driving Cars

10   Revenue Estimates Of AI Self-Driving Cars

11   Survivalists and AI Self-Driving Cars

This title is available via Amazon and other book sellers

Companion Book By This Author

AI Self-Driving Cars
Autonomy

by Dr. Lance B. Eliot, MBA, PhD

Chapter Title

1 Eliot Framework for AI Self-Driving Cars

2 Your Bucket List and AI Self-Driving Cars

3 Highway Stunts and AI Self-Driving Cars

4 Future Wonderment and AI Self-Driving Cars

5 AI On-The-Fly Learning and AI Self-Driving Cars

6 Level 4 and Level 5 of AI Self-Driving Cars

7 Explaining Key Acronyms of AI Self-Driving Cars

8 Walmart Edge Computing and AI Self-Driving Cars

9 Stonehenge Lessons and AI Self-Driving Cars

10 Levels of Autonomy Feud and AI Self-Driving Cars

11 Hide and Escape Via AI Self-Driving Cars

This title is available via Amazon and other book sellers

Companion Book By This Author

AI Driverless Cars
Transmutation

by Dr. Lance B. Eliot, MBA, PhD

Chapter Title

1 Eliot Framework for AI Self-Driving Cars

2 Backup Drivers and AI Self-Driving Cars

3 Teaching Kids about AI Self-Driving Cars

4 Hand-off Problem and AI Self-Driving Cars

5 Racial Bias and AI Self-Driving Cars

6 AI Consciousness and AI Self-Driving Cars

7 Machine Learning Riddles and AI Self-Driving Cars

8 Spurring Financial Literacy via AI Self-Driving Cars

9 GM Cruise Minivan and AI Self-Driving Cars

10 Car Off Cliff Lessons and AI Self-Driving Cars

11 Daughter Prank and AI Self-Driving Cars

This title is available via Amazon and other book sellers

Companion Book By This Author

AI Driverless Cars Potentiality

by Dr. Lance B. Eliot, MBA, PhD

Chapter Title

1 Eliot Framework for AI Self-Driving Cars

2 Russian Values and AI Self-Driving Cars

3 Friendships Uplift and AI Self-Driving Cars

4 Dogs Driving and AI Self-Driving Cars

5 Hypodermic Needles and AI Self-Driving Cars

6 Sharing Self-Driving Tech Is Not Likely

7 Uber Driver "Kidnapper" Is Self-Driving Car Lesson

8 Gender Driving Biases In AI Self-Driving Cars

9 Slain Befriended Dolphins Are Self-Driving Car Lesson

10 Analysis Of AI In Government Report

11 Mobility Frenzy and AI Self-Driving Cars

This title is available via Amazon and other book sellers

ABOUT THE AUTHOR

Dr. Lance B. Eliot, MBA, PhD is the CEO of Techbruim, Inc. and Executive Director of the Cybernetic AI Self-Driving Car Institute and has over twenty years of industry experience including serving as a corporate officer in a billion dollar firm and was a partner in a major executive services firm. He is also a serial entrepreneur having founded, ran, and sold several high-tech related businesses. He previously hosted the popular radio show *Technotrends* that was also available on American Airlines flights via their in-flight audio program. Author or co-author of a dozen books and over 400 articles, he has made appearances on CNN, and has been a frequent speaker at industry conferences.

A former professor at the University of Southern California (USC), he founded and led an innovative research lab on Artificial Intelligence in Business. Known as the "AI Insider" his writings on AI advances and trends has been widely read and cited. He also previously served on the faculty of the University of California Los Angeles (UCLA), and was a visiting professor at other major universities. He was elected to the International Board of the Society for Information Management (SIM), a prestigious association of over 3,000 high-tech executives worldwide.

He has performed extensive community service, including serving as Senior Science Adviser to the Vice Chair of the Congressional Committee on Science & Technology. He has served on the Board of the OC Science & Engineering Fair (OCSEF), where he is also has been a Grand Sweepstakes judge, and likewise served as a judge for the Intel International SEF (ISEF). He served as the Vice Chair of the Association for Computing Machinery (ACM) Chapter, a prestigious association of computer scientists. Dr. Eliot has been a shark tank judge for the USC Mark Stevens Center for Innovation on start-up pitch competitions, and served as a mentor for several incubators and accelerators in Silicon Valley and Silicon Beach. He served on several Boards and Committees at USC, including having served on the Marshall Alumni Association (MAA) Board in Southern California.

Dr. Eliot holds a PhD from USC, MBA, and Bachelor's in Computer Science, and earned the CDP, CCP, CSP, CDE, and CISA certifications. Born and raised in Southern California, and having traveled and lived internationally, he enjoys scuba diving, surfing, and sailing.

ADDENDUM

AI Driverless Cars Potentiality

Practical Advances in Artificial Intelligence (AI) and Machine Learning

By

Dr. Lance B. Eliot, MBA, PhD

―――――

For supplemental materials of this book, visit:

www.ai-selfdriving-cars.guru

For special orders of this book, contact:

LBE Press Publishing

Email: LBE.Press.Publishing@gmail.com

www.ingramcontent.com/pod-product-compliance
Lightning Source LLC
Chambersburg PA
CBHW051047050326
40690CB00006B/623